Canon and Creativity

Robert Alter

Canon and Creativity

modern writing and the authority of scripture

Yale University Press   New Haven and London

Published with assistance from the Mary Cady Tew Memorial Fund.

"The Dead of the Desert" is reprinted from *Chaim Nahman Bialik: Selected Poems,* translated by Ruth Nevo, copyright © 1981 by Dvir Ltd. Reprinted with the permission of Dvir Ltd.

Library of Congress Cataloging-in-Publication Data

Alter, Robert.

Canon and creativity : modern writing and the authority of scripture / Robert Alter.

p. cm.

Includes bibliographical references and index.

ISBN 0-300-08424-2 (cloth : alk. paper)

1. Literature, Modern—20th century—History and criticism. 2. Literature, Modern—19th century—History and criticism. 3. Canon (Literature) 4. Bible and literature.

PN771 .A69   2000

809'.04—dc21   00-035168

A catalogue record for this book is available from the British Library.

10 9 8 7 6 5 4 3 2 1

For Yehuda Amichai
with abiding affection

contents

Contents

acknowledgments

The initial prompting for the idea of this book came to me when my friend David Biale asked me to write an essay on the Bible and the canon for a volume entitled *Insider/Outsider* that he was coediting. I had my doubts at first, wondering whether the very topic was a tautology, but the more I looked into it, the more I began to think that canonicity was a many-sided thing with rather interesting cultural consequences. Chapter 1 here is a revised version of the essay I wrote on that general topic. When I was subsequently invited by Yale University to deliver the Rosenzweig Lectures during the spring of 1999, I decided to apply some of the notions I had developed on the continuing life of the biblical canon to three exemplary modern writers, with an eye both to the nature of the canon and to literary modernism. Chapters 2, 3, and 4 are based on the lectures I gave at Yale. I would like to thank Paula Hyman and the faculty of the Program in Jewish

Studies at Yale for their kind hospitality during my stay in New Haven. I am also grateful to the alert and receptive audiences at the lectures: several of their astute questions helped shape my final formulations.

A draft version was read by my Berkeley friends Michael Bernstein and Tom Rosenmeyer: both their suggestions and their encouragement were important to me. My thanks to Janet Livingstone for her meticulous preparation of the typescript. Incidental research expenses were covered by funds from the Class of 1937 Chair in Comparative Literature at the University of California at Berkeley.

introduction
Canons, Canonicity, and Literary Expression

*O*ver the last quarter of the twentieth century, the term *canon,* which previously had been restricted to the body of Sacred Scripture approved by ecclesiastical authority, attained general currency in academic circles as a designation for the corpus of secular literary works implicitly or explicitly endorsed by established cultural authority as worthy of preservation through reading and study. In a curious way, usage had come full circle. In the Hellenistic era, grammarians who assembled lists of required works for their students called any author worthy of inclusion *kanonikos,* "one who comes up to the standard." But before long the Church made *canon* its virtually exclusive property, and that is how matters rested until the late twentieth century. There was an obvious polemic advantage in the extension of the term from sacred to profane. It helped expose the ways in which cultures achieve internal coherence through a politics of exclusion, and it thus laid the grounds for a critical and cultural reconsideration of excluded works and writers. The evident gain of such reconsideration has been an enlarged sense of our literary heritage, which now seems somewhat more diverse and multifaceted than it did a couple of generations back, when central works of criticism flaunted such confident titles as *The Great Tradition* and *Modern Poetry and the Tradition*. All along, however, the flip side of this polemic revelation has been polemic exaggeration. The notion of a literary canon implies some rough analogy to a council of church fathers or rabbinic sages deciding what goes in and what stays out on the basis of doctrinal or ideological principle. In fact, the secular canon through the ages has been a quirky and various thing, its borders and perceived centers shifting according to changing taste and intellectual fashion at least as much as on ideological grounds. Exclusion by gender, ethnicity, or social class has by no means been so relentless as is often claimed: half a century ago, the canonicity of Jane Austen and George Eliot had long been firmly in place, and a lesser figure such as Aphra Behn, the seventeenth-century playwright, poet, and fiction writer, was already a fixture on graduate reading lists, decades before she lent her name to a journal of feminist studies.

The great virtue of Harold Bloom's 1994 study *The Western Canon* is that it vigorously rejects the notion that the canon — Bloom, like all of us, is now stuck with the term — is chiefly a mechanism of ideological coercion. Instead, he argues that literary works fight their way to canonicity through their strangeness, their originality, their power to make us see the world in new and surprising ways. The major difference I have with Bloom's conception of the canonical is that it depends so heavily on a tense clash of wills between writers and their masterful predecessors, assuming the model of Oedipal conflict to which he has long been committed. The exuberant playfulness of art is given short shrift in this account, and there is little notion that literary tradition might often offer enlivening occasions for continuity as well as serving as a battleground for warring creative egos. (In the discussion of Joyce's *Ulysses* that concludes this study, I shall try to highlight both the pleasurable playfulness and the strong sense of continuity with which a new work may insert itself in the existing canon.)

There will no doubt continue to be debate

about how the literary canon is constituted, and further thought might well be given to the question of whether in fact the idea of a literary canon is a coherent and useful concept. In one respect, it is unfortunate that this debate should take place mainly within the precincts of the academy, for academic people tend to see the world largely in terms of their own institutional situation, and thus imagine that the canon is more or less determined by what is included in course syllabi. Indeed, that may explain the appeal of adopting from ecclesiastical history the notion of the canon as an approved list of authoritative works. As a critic of modern literature who has also devoted considerable attention to the biblical canon itself, I was led by the counterclaims and confusions of the debate over the literary canon to reconsider what canonicity might mean in the strict scriptural sense. On reflection, it strikes me that the canonicity of the Bible is by no means the simple and assured phenomenon of enshrining doctrine in text that it is often assumed to be. There are odd and instructive anomalies of inclusion in the biblical canon—especially in the Hebrew Bible—as there are in the secular canon. These anomalies make one wonder whether the motives of the original canonizers were in fact limited to considerations of doctrine and institutional cohesiveness, and whether the life lived by canon through the many generations of its perpetuators went beyond its utility as a vehicle for theological truths. In my initial chapter, I shall try to open up these questions of canonicity by looking first at the Hebrew Bible proper and then at the vigorous and often surprising afterlife it has led in postbiblical Hebrew literature, both sacred and profane. As the special but illuminating case of Hebrew literature demonstrates, a canon can be much more flexible, and less ideologically binding, than prevalent conceptions allow.

A canon is above all a transhistorical textual community. Knowledge of the received texts and recourse to them constitute the community, but the texts do not have a single, authoritative meaning, however much the established spokesmen for the canon at any given moment may claim that is the case. After all, even within the community of traditional believers, the biblical canon has been imagined to endorse as a matter of divine revelation rationalism, mysticism, nationalism, universalism, asceticism, sensualism, determinism, free will, and a good deal else. Modern writers, then, merely push to the next step this process of extending the range of meanings of the textual community in which they participate when they use the biblical canon, as we shall see, to express vitalistic pantheism, or an individual fate of hapless victimhood, or a vision of cosmic pitilessness, or a notion of eternal recurrence.

The aim of the discussion I have undertaken here is twofold. On the one hand, I want to explore the dynamics of canonicity, attending to the ways in which the exemplary canonical corpus of the Western tradition, the Bible, is assimilated and imaginatively reused by poets and writers of fiction. And because all the major examples considered involve intersections of secular—perhaps one should say heterodox—literary expression with the Bible, some better understanding may be attained not only of biblical canonicity but of literary canonicity as well. On the other hand, because the three writers discussed in detail all flourished in the great period of ferment and innovation of literary modernism—schematically, the first quarter of the twentieth century—a scrutiny of their sundry energetic engagements with the Bible may throw some light on the range and nature of the modernist enterprise. The rapid trajectory traced here from Kafka to Bialik to Joyce, and from German to Hebrew to English, in fact suggests that *range* is a better term for modernism than *nature*, that modernism is not one thing but a cluster of related and also divergent cultural trends. One of these three writers, Bialik, is hardly a modernist at all in regard to literary form, but, as I shall try to show, the radical spiritual project of his remarkable mythic poem "The Dead of the Desert" participates in an underlying cultural task undertaken by many of the more familiar and more readily identifiable modernists.

Most of us tend to associate modernism with iconoclasm, and there is a good deal of warrant for making that connection: poets, following the precedent of such late-nineteenth-century trailblazers as Rimbaud and Mallarmé, cultivated elusive obliquities, startling discontinuities, surprises of figuration, structural jaggedness; novelists abandoned linear narration, substituted chains of elliptic mental associations for the lucid and orderly delineation of character and scene, and in a few striking instances treated the restraints of realism itself as an outmoded convention. But if the label of iconoclasm has a certain seductive plausibility for modernism, it by no means provides an adequate characterization of all the major instances. Is Proust, for example, really an iconoclastic writer? It is true that his endlessly patient reflectiveness, inscribed in the very convolutions of his syntax, slows the forward movement of narration to an unprecedented leisurely pace, but he seems to be extravagantly elaborating the essayistic and analytic modes of the nineteenth-century realist novel rather than shattering old formal modes. Modernism often looks like a paradoxical amalgam of iconoclasm and hypertraditionalism. (An essential difference from postmodernism may be that the postmodernists generally discard or lampoon the traditionalism.)

The engagement of modern writers with the Bible is especially instructive because it cuts sharply two ways. They frequently translate biblical motifs and themes into radically redefining new contexts, and, as we shall see in the case of Bialik, their stance toward the Bible can sometimes be positively combative. At the same time, the Bible remains for them a value-laden, imaginatively energizing body of texts, helping make possible the novels and poems they write through the powers of expression and vision that inhere in it. Kafka was a thoroughly Europeanized modern Jew struggling, perhaps futilely, with the idea of belief and the tradition that embodied it. Bialik had escaped from the world of East European Jewish piety in late adolescence, carrying with him a mixed burden of guilt, intermittent nostalgia, and bitterness toward it. Joyce, educated by Jesuits, fashioned an essentially aesthetic artistic ideal that blended an earthy paganism with certain motifs and ideas drawn from both Judaism and Christianity. These three exemplary instances, then, are chosen from very disparate points on the cultural and credal map. None of the three embraced the biblical canon with a believer's theological certitude, but, as their works attest, the canonicity of the Bible was acutely palpable to them, imaginatively available to them, perhaps in some ways that it might not be to the conventional believer. The inventive and at times disorienting use of the Bible in their writing is a vivid manifestation of the dialectic of iconoclasm and traditionalism that informs a good deal of modernist writing.

Let me illustrate this potency of the canonical text in what at first may seem to be a drastically postcanonical historical moment with one of the most profound and spectacular invocations of the Bible in modernist fiction, William Faulkner's *Absalom, Absalom!* Faulkner liked to say that he reread the Bible (of course, in the King James Version) from one end to another every year. Whether or not this was literally true, it is clear that the imaginative texture of the Bible pervaded his decidedly unbiblical prose to a degree that is matched among American novelists perhaps only by Melville. David, Absalom, and the rape of Tamar are never explicitly alluded to in Faulkner's novel, though the title directs us to an elaborate set of correspondences of plot and theme between the ancient and the modern stories, while emphatically marked allusions in the novel to Greek tragedy coordinate it with the Bible in a manner akin to Joyce's synoptic perspective on Greek epic and the Bible in *Ulysses*. Faulkner's implicit reading of the Book of Samuel is deeply penetrating, for he understands that the narrative of the founding of the Davidic dynasty is, paradoxically, the haunting story of the fall of the house of David and of the unfolding of an implacable curse on David, and thus it can serve beautifully as an analogue for the story of Thomas Sutpen, would-be founder of a Southern dynasty whose overweening ambition is disastrously thwarted by a fatal flaw in the man. The intricate correspondences (as well as the ironic divergences) between Faulkner's plot and the biblical one are fascinating to contemplate, but what I want to stress here is how an underlying relation between story and historical reality in Faulkner's novel is enabled by the Bible. It is this that I had in mind when I referred to the presence of the imaginative texture of the Bible in Faulkner's writing. Let me briefly explain.

On the most readily definable level, the Bible gives Faulkner a certain lexicon for imagining, even for conceptualizing, history and, more specifically, historical catastrophe. Faulkner's trademark vocabulary is polysyllabic and extravagantly Greco-Latinate, exhibiting a fondness for elusive and paradoxical abstractions that is distinctly unbiblical. But *Absalom, Absalom!* is also marked by the recurrence of a set of plain English terms redolent of the King James Version, such as *blessing, curse* (far more of the latter), *land, seed, flesh and bone,* and *blood.* These terms provide Faulkner the means to conceive what I would describe as a biblicizing relation to historical reality in the American South: the *land* beckons seductively as the destined arena for the fulfillment of divine or self-assumed promise; *seed,* the biologically concrete manifestation of personal continuity, is the necessary agency for the realization of the promise through the time of history; *curse* is the inexorable frustration, triggered by moral failure, of those hopes of lasting dominion in this land of milk and honey; *flesh and bone* is the palpable realm of the family that proves to be the principal vehicle of frustration; *blood* is family again, and guilt, and, above all, the continuing fate of violence through which the curse is implemented.

This biblical lexicon figures in a novel that is, famously, an intricate construction of sundry tales told or invented by different narrators about a terrible shared past which at once haunts and escapes all the storytellers. Precisely in this regard, the Bible, that long chain of age-old tales pondered by this American writer year after year, is a compelling model for the novelist's own project. Here is Mr. Compson trying to explain to his son Quentin how the world of the Sutpens, and, more specifically, that fatal moment between 1861 and 1865 when the South with all its illusions foundered, continues to resist the anxious scrutiny of its lineal descendants: "We have a few old mouth-to-mouth tales; we exhume from old trunks and boxes and drawers, letters without salutation or signature, in which men and women who once lived and breathed are now merely initials or nicknames out of some now incomprehensible affection which sound to us like Sanskrit or Choctaw; we see dimly people, the people in whose living blood and seed we ourselves lay dormant and waiting, in this shad-

owy attenuation of time possessing now heroic proportions, performing their acts of simple passion
and simple violence, impervious to time and inex-
plicable."[1]

The splendid extravagance of the prose, even
if a touch muted here, is unmistakably Faulknerian
—the panoply of overlapping terms for elusiveness
and impenetrability ("impervious to time and in-
explicable," and in the unquoted conclusion of this
same paragraph, "indecipherable," "inscrutable"),
the Baroque relish for joining Latinate polysyllabic words with more homespun Anglo-Saxon
ones ("this shadowy attenuation of time"), the repeated emphasis on dim or fleeting images, the
syntactic cascade of mutually reinforcing phrases
and clauses. This is a style that harks back to the
seventeenth-century prose of Robert Burton and
Thomas Browne, emphatically different in sensi-
bility from the framers of the King James Version
who were their approximate contemporaries. And
yet, at the imaginative center of this passage stands
a pair of quintessentially biblical terms, "blood and
seed," which signals the ultimately biblical conception of history, memory, and narrative that informs *Absalom, Absalom!* However sharply etched
the individual characters, human destiny is imag-

ined as a collective, historical experience, effected through a biological connection between generations—hence Mr. Compson's troubled perception that he and his kin are directly sprung from the living blood and seed of those vaguely glimpsed figures from the past. Equally crucial to the power of biblical intertextuality in Faulkner's representation of the American South is his insight into the role played by history in the biblical narrative. The ancient Israelites were a history-haunted people, and some eminent scholars have seen in the David story the very beginnings of genuine history writing in the Western tradition. Faulkner, I would suggest, understood matters differently, and perhaps more deeply. For the Hebrew audience of antiquity, nothing could have been more important than establishing the truth ("facts" would be an anachronistic concept) about the founding of their monarchy, a monarchy with seeming divine underwriting that nevertheless split in two after only one generation and eventually fell ignominiously to foreign conquerors. Yet the purportedly authoritative account in the Book of Samuel is itself in some ways contradictory, and revolves around a David who is a man of contradictions, perhaps ultimately unfathomable, quite like Thomas Sutpen. And though

Faulkner in this passage scarcely has textual criticism of the Bible in mind, the text-critical scholars have made us generally aware that the biblical story itself is an elaborate stitching-together of sundry documents and scraps of scrolls — the ancient Near Eastern equivalent of the contents of those antiquated trunks and boxes — joined with literary versions of "old mouth-to-mouth tales." Faulkner, for example, may never have noticed that Goliath is, memorably, reported to be slain by David in the middle of 1 Samuel and, more cryptically, said to be killed by a certain Elhanan toward the end of 2 Samuel, but it is a clash between competing versions of the same tale that this inventor of multiple narrators might have relished.

The Hebrew imagination, as early as its founding biblical phase, laid the grounds for what could be called a culture of exegesis. Prose narrative was its first instrument for expressing the reality of the nation's historical experience, but unlike the lucid, leisurely narrative of Homer's sunlit world, it is a kind of abrupt story that turns on dark places, that is riddled with unsettling enigmas — in the instance of the text that stands behind Faulkner's novel, incestuous rape, fratricide, insurrection, a bloody struggle for succession, and the spectacle of a once-powerful man on the throne who seems to have lost the capacity to wield power. The primary narrative is, as we have noted, composite, a redactor's orchestration of tensions among divergent or even clashing views of the represented figures and events. It is thus both a report of what happened and a puzzling, an interpreter's struggle, over the reported action. One readily understands how such a narrative would generate three thousand years of exegesis, with no end in sight. (Gershom Scholem's idea that the intrinsic need to be grasped through exegesis is one of the primary traits of the canonical text has deep resonance in this connection.) Faulkner keenly intuits the exegetical character of biblical narrative as it strives to address crucial junctures of a history that is traumatic, ungraspable, yet continually mesmerizing. In the sentence after the one where our excerpt breaks off, he has Mr. Compson liken the central figures of his story to "a chemical formula exhumed along with the letters from that forgotten chest, carefully, the paper old and faded and falling to pieces, the writing faded, almost indecipherable, yet meaningful; . . . you re-read, tedious and intent, poring, making sure you have forgotten nothing, made no miscalculations . . ."—and yet the words refuse to cohere into definitive meaning, refuse to yield the palpable presence of the lived lives that have determined the lives of those who come after them.

Faulkner, as a bold visionary of the dark side of modernism (Joyce expresses the bright side, as we shall have occasion to see), is by no means restricted to a biblical intertext as analogue and precedent for his vision. In *Absalom, Absalom!* as I have observed, Greek tragedy also has some importance as a literary model for representing, in the memorable concluding phrase of the paragraph I have been quoting, the "horrible and bloody mischancing of human affairs." When we consider Joyce, I shall speculate about the cultural implications of such bracketing of the Bible with Greek literature. For the moment, I want to point up what the example of Faulkner tells us about the canonical power of the Bible for secular literature in an era no longer, at least for many of the writers, an age of faith. It is worth insisting on the concept of power because the imagination of the latter-day writer, as Faulkner shows, remains very much under the sway of the literary force of the biblical text, and it proves to be a force that empowers his own writing.

The Bible in part seizes the imagination of the modern writer because of his acute consciousness of it as a body of founding texts, marking out one of the primary possibilities of representing the human condition and the nature of historical experience for all the eras of Western culture that have followed antiquity. This recourse to founding texts makes special sense if one recalls the impulse to fundamental cultural stock taking or self-recapitulation that characterizes a good deal of modernist writing. What a modernist may take from the Bible is not necessarily revealed truth or theological principle; but, as I shall argue in my first chapter, the canonicity of the Bible all along inhered not only in the divine origins attributed to the texts. Faulkner, like the other modern writers whose work we shall be pondering, saw something true and deep in the Bible that spoke to his own sense of the world, though it is not anything that Aquinas or Maimonides would have been likely to see in the Bible. Faulkner's relation to Scripture, like that of his literary contemporaries, illustrates how a canon is a dynamic transhistorical textual community and not a timeless inscription of fixed meanings. "The past," Walter Benjamin wrote in the fifth of his "Theses on the Philosophy of History," "can be seized only as an image which flashes up at the instant when it can be recognized and is never seen again." The notion of the past, and, in our context, of the biblical texts that represent it, as a fleeting or stroboscopic image is quite Faulknerian — coincidentally, Benjamin, who almost certainly did not read Faulkner, wrote these words just four years after the publication of *Absalom, Absalom!* — though Faulkner might have been skeptical about whether the past can ever really be seized, even momentarily. We try to grab hold of the past, Benjamin goes on to say, "as it flashes up in a moment of danger." The general principle he underscores, with the task of the historian in mind, is equally valid for imaginative writers and the way they participate in their transhistorical textual community, perpetuating through their work the life of the canon: "For every image of the past that is not recognized by the present as one of its own concerns threatens to disappear irretrievably."[2] The modern writers we shall scrutinize in the pages that follow provide in their work potent antidotes to the disappearance of the inherited canon from effective cultural memory precisely because they recognize in it eloquent images of their own urgent concerns, even in cases where they feel obliged to question or actually challenge the evident values of the biblical authors. If their writing in certain respects unsettles the canon, makes us read it differently, invites us to imagine its cultural role in altered terms, they also reaffirm the continuing authority of the canon as a resource of collective memory and as a guide for contemplating the dense tangle of human fate.

1

The Double Canonicity of the Hebrew Bible

*O*ne might reasonably assume that the Bible provides contemporary cultural criticism with the very paradigm for the idea of a canon. Indeed, as late as 1955, the *Oxford English Dictionary*, while registering no application whatever of the term to works of secular literature, offers as its only entry relevant to current usage this thoroughly unambiguous definition: "the list of books of the Bible accepted by the Christian Church as genuine and inspired." The Christian character of the canon taken for granted in this definition is worth noting, for, as I shall try to show in detail, the canonicity of the Bible for Jews from late antiquity to the modern era has in part meant something analagous but also rather different. The authoritative certitude fixed in the canon according to this dictionary definition vividly illustrates the tendentiousness in the recent widespread adoption of the term for secular literary works, fostering as it does a tacit notion of a kind of synod of cultural authorities who have dictated a list of "genuine and inspired" writers, excluding proponents of the wrong ideological or aesthetic bent or the wrong gender or ethnicity. In fact, the reasons why certain works become popular beyond their own times and are anthologized, reprinted, cherished by readers, even included in curricula, are more complicated, more fluid, and more interestingly multifarious than the ecclesiastical model of a canon suggests. But the canonicity of the Hebrew Bible itself proves to be, on closer consideration, more ambiguous, and also more overdetermined, than is allowed by this idea of a list of genuine and inspired works.

We have only an imperfect, highly inferential notion of how the canonization of Hebrew Scriptures actually took place—apparently, by stages —among Jews sometime around the turn of the Christian era. The talmudic account of a kind of parliamentary vote on a list of canonical works by the Sanhedrin on a single day in Yavneh in 90 C.E. has been questioned by recent scholars and may well be a schematization of a more complicated historical process.[1] The Torah was evidently accepted as canonical by the time of Ezra the Scribe (later

sixth century B.C.E.), for he could not have pre-
scribed its reading as a public ritual without assuming, or at any rate effectively imposing, such acceptance (though we have no way of being sure that the
Torah he decreed for reading was textually identi-
cal with that of later tradition). The Prophets, including the narrative books designated the Former
Prophets, appear to have become canonical over
the next four centuries, as evidence from the Dead
Sea Scrolls and elsewhere suggests. So far so good,
a proponent of the idea of canon as a list of genuine and inspired books might say. The Torah, after
all, gives us an account of the origins of the world,
the formation of the people of Israel, and its divine election and redemption from slavery, together
with the body of laws—moral, civil, and cultic—
that is to govern it. The Former Prophets continue
the story of God's covenanted people to the end of
the First Commonwealth. The Latter Prophets explicitly represent themselves as carriers of God's
message to Israel (the so-called messenger formula,
"thus saith the Lord," is often invoked in their writings), articulating in a new way the moral implications of the Covenant and making a set of assertions
about the future course of history.

The third large unit, however, of what became the Hebrew Bible, the miscellaneous Writings *(Ketuvim)*, raises questions about any clear-cut ideological or theological criteria for the constitution of the canon. The Writings include, after all: a kind of carnivalesque political fairy tale in which God's name is never mentioned (Esther); a profound challenge to traditional notions of divine justice and reward and punishment that concludes with a radical revision of the anthropocentric vision of creation in Genesis (Job); an exuberantly sensual celebration of the pleasures of young—and evidently unmarried—love, again with no mention of God (the Song of Songs); a brooding series of poetic-philosophic reflections on the futility of all human endeavor and desire and the leveling prospect of cyclical recurrence in all things (Ecclesiastes). How did such wayward or nearly heretical texts come to be part of the Hebrew Bible? A provisional answer may help us understand more clearly the role played in the cultural life of later Jews, and perhaps not just Jews, not only by these "problematic" books but by the entire Hebrew Bible, and may give us a clearer notion of how canons in general are made.

Let me begin by observing a rudimentary fact that has had more far-reaching consequences than is generally realized: the Jews, from late antiquity to relatively recent times, read the Bible, unlike all other peoples, in the original Hebrew. There are some significant exceptions to this rule. The Hellenized Jewish community of Alexandria in the last centuries of the pre-Christian era seems to have been dependent on the Greek translation of the Bible. The wide dissemination of the Aramaic Targums (paraphrastic translations read aloud in synagogues together with the Hebrew originals) in the early Christian era is a clear indication that large numbers of Jews, in a time and place when Aramaic had displaced Hebrew as the vernacular, needed a translation, at least as a pony for understanding the original. It would be extravagant, moreover, to imagine that the educational system at any time or place in the history of the Diaspora produced universal literate comprehension of Hebrew among Jewish males. It is likely that quite typically an ordinary person would end up only with a dependable ability to sound out the Hebrew letters on the page and identify the meanings of some primary items of vocabulary. Nevertheless, anyone who could be considered truly educated in traditional Jewish society would have been intimately familiar with the Bible in its original language; and

indeed, though after the first few years of school-
ing the curriculum centered on the Talmud, not
the Bible, there is considerable literary evidence
that a nearly verbatim recall of the entire Hebrew
Bible was by no means an unusual accomplishment.
(One might think of the analogy of Russian culture, in which many educated people managed to
get much of Pushkin by heart.) The group that
achieved Hebrew literacy may have been an elite,
but it was by no means a tiny one. My guess is that
the proportion of the male Jewish population in
eleventh-century Andalusia or eighteenth-century
Lithuania that could read Genesis and Job in the
original easily exceeded the proportion of people in
eighteenth-century English society who read Virgil
in the original, at a time when English poetry was
modeled on Augustan verse.

It is obvious that a great work of literature can
have a profound effect on readers in translation, as
the enormous impact of Homer, Dante, and Shakespeare in many languages demonstrates. But it is
equally obvious that the tonalities, the associations,
the order of imaginative authority, shift, usually
with some palpable diminution, when a work mani-
festing great verbal mastery is transferred from one
language to another. Such shifts are particularly

drastic in the case of the Hebrew Bible because most of the languages into which it has been translated are so different from Hebrew in structure, idiom, sound, and semantic coloration. The effect of reading the Bible in its original language is, I think, paramount in the inclusion in the canon of the four books I have mentioned that ended up in the miscellaneous Writings. Apart from any considerations of ideology, if the Jews of late antiquity had read these texts in Greek or Aramaic, I think it is rather unlikely that they would have felt impelled to put them in the Bible.

Why would a book that either rejects doctrinal consensus or pays no attention to doctrine be taken into the supposedly doctrinal canon? The two most plausible explanations—literary power and sheer popularity—in part overlap, in part complement each other. Both Esther and the Song of Songs are self-evidently popular works. Esther would have had wide appeal because it provided the rationale for a new, attractively festive holiday, Purim, while playing on feelings of national pride and solidarity in an inventive satiric narrative. Neither of these considerations is related to the language in which the story is written. The liveliness of the tale, however, is strikingly enhanced by the Hebrew in which it is conveyed, with its playfulness, its puns, its descriptive vividness so different from earlier Hebrew prose, and its colorful borrowings from the Persian. (Such considerations at first carried little weight in some pietistic circles: the absence of any fragment of Esther from Qumran — the only biblical book not represented in the library of the Dead Sea sectarians — suggests that as late as the first or second century B.C.E. there were groups that rejected its canonicity.) The popular character of the Song of Songs is attested by the early rabbinic objection in the Tosefta (Sanhedrin 12:10) to a common practice of singing it, with plainly erotic intention, in places of public revelry. But the popular attraction of the Song surely derives not merely from its subject — the wasteland of the extracanonical through the ages is littered with erotica — but from its extraordinary poetic vehicle, which in the lushness of its imagery, its subtle musicality, its sense of drama, its fusion of delicate sensuality and verbal wit, turns biblical Hebrew into an instrument of enchantment.

The other two problem-books, Job and Ecclesiastes, raise the question of ideology and canon more directly because both are philosophic challenges to views generally accepted in the dominant body of beliefs of ancient Israel. It is not unreasonable to surmise that the very profundity of the challenges—a profundity that would have spoken to an intellectual elite more than to a popular audience—arrested the attention of certain Hebrew readers and drove them to argue for the inclusion of these texts in the canon. If that was in fact the case, it would indicate that ideological consensus among the makers of the Jewish canon was less a matter of party-line agreement than one might imagine, that the canon makers were willing to tolerate a certain spectrum of outlooks, or perhaps felt that it was salutary for the consecrated literature to incorporate some dialectic elements of autocritique. But an equally important aspect of the appeal of both these books is their unique power as instances of literary Hebrew, a power that manifestly focuses the boldness of the philosophic critique they articulate. The metaphoric vigor of the poetry of Job, its stunning ability to inscribe pain and outrage and cosmic vision in taut, muscular language, give it an awesome intensity of a kind attained by only a few other works—*Oedipus the King, The Inferno, King Lear,* perhaps a few poems of Celan's—in the whole Western poetic tradition. Ecclesiastes, moving back and forth between highly rhythmic prose and passages

of poetry, is a haunting evocation of the hazy insub-
stantiality of ambition and hope that has a mesmerizing effect in the Hebrew because of its echoing
cadences, verse after verse registering in sound the
writer's underlying sense that all things are weary-
ingly repeated in an endless cycle of futility.

I don't mean to propose that ultimately what
the Hebrew Bible represents is the twenty-four
best-selling books of ancient Hebrew literature.
The limits of the canon were, after all, defined by a
system of belief, even if it was in a few respects surprisingly flexible, and there doubtless were works
composed in Hebrew in the biblical period that had
no chance of admission to the canon because they
stood outside the system, or addressed concerns
entirely irrelevant to it, even by way of challenge.
(We have no way of knowing the nature of the lost
books mentioned in the Bible: the Book of Yashar,
the Book of the Battles of YHWH, the Chronicles
of the Kings of Judea, and the Chronicles of the
Kings of Israel. Perhaps the first two were deemed
too mythical in character for retention even in the
precanonical stage of anthologizing the national literature, and the last two may have expressed too
limited a dynastic view of historical events.) Nevertheless, the stylistic and imaginative authority of

the works that became canonical must have played a role in the desire to preserve them in the national legacy—and, conversely, it seems plausible that there were Hebrew texts excluded from the canon not for doctrinal reasons but because they were inferior as works of literature. The soaring, and searing, poetry of Job, the lovely lyricism of the Song of Songs, were so keenly appreciated by the ancient audience that it was unwilling to have them lost to posterity, for all the theological radicalism of the former and the sensual secularity of the latter.

The case, moreover, was not fundamentally different for ancient Hebrew texts that posed no challenge to doctrine. Genesis might be thought of as a perfectly "orthodox" work, authoritatively defining the hierarchy of creation and the election of Israel, but it is also one of the supreme achievements of narrative art in all of ancient literature, on the level of style, story, dialogue, and the complex representation of character and theme. The Hebrew audience in the Second Commonwealth period no doubt readily assented to the canonical status of the redacted text we call Genesis because it consciously viewed the book as a veracious report of creation and national origins, but it is hard to imagine that the ancient audience did not also respond with deep approbation to the brilliant literary artistry of the book (which surely was not exercised by the authors and editors merely for their own amusement, in disregard of any audience). This double responsiveness to Scripture read in the richness of its original language has continued to manifest itself in the Jewish relation to the Bible through the ages. The nearly ubiquitous presence of allusions to the Bible in postbiblical Hebrew literature is a major index of this binocular vision of the Bible: the allusions occur because the Bible provides later Hebrew writers a thick concordance of phrases, motifs, and symbols that encode a set of theological, historical, and national values (a canon in the strict sense of the *O.E.D.*); and the allusions occur, as I shall try to show, because the Bible in Hebrew speaks resonantly, even to the most pious readers, as a collection of great works of literature.

The history of English literature from the seventeenth century affords an approximate but instructive parallel to this phenomenon. The magisterial achievement of the King James Version (whatever its imperfections and its inaccuracies) profoundly impressed itself not only on the community of the pious but on most of those who wrote literature. English literary style as it evolved is scarcely imaginable without reference to the King James Version. It is deeply imprinted not only in the language of such intently religious poets as George Herbert and Emily Dickenson but also in writers beyond the pale of traditional belief as different from each other as Hemingway, Joyce, and D. H. Lawrence.

The persistent power of this second, literary canonicity for readers of the Hebrew Bible, including those in ages dominated by doctrine, helps explain one of the great enigmas of Jewish cultural history—the dramatic rebirth of a secular literature in Hebrew, twice: first in late-tenth-century Spain, initiating a rich and varied tradition that would continue down to eighteenth-century Italy, and then in Central and Eastern Europe, beginning falteringly in Enlightenment Prussia and reaching artistic maturity in Russia toward the end of the nineteenth century. A necessary condition of the first of these rebirths was a conscious return of the Andalusian Hebrew poets to the language of the Bible, in competitive imitation of the Arabic poets who vaunted the purity of Quranic style of their verse. Literary historians often represent this biblicizing impulse of the Andalusian poets as chiefly a linguistic undertaking: with a clarity of understanding derived from the new Semitic philology of the era, the poets could cut away the grammatical and morphological excrescences of antecedent liturgical poetry, go back to the precision of biblical usages, and mine the Bible for vocabulary and idiom. Although all this is true, what is equally impressive is the way they evince in poem after poem a subtle responsiveness to the literary artistry and the imaginative worlds of the biblical writers. The celebration of nature, the expression of physical passion, the articulation of loneliness and personal loss, the broodings on mortality and the ephemerality of all things in this extraordinary body of secular poetry would be inconceivable without the poets' profound imaginative experience of Psalms, the Song of Songs, Job, Ecclesiastes, Proverbs, and other biblical texts as works of literature.

What I want to stress is that this sort of imaginative experience of Scripture did not suddenly begin in tenth- and eleventh-century Córdoba and Granada and Seville because members of the Jewish cultural elite there picked up from the surrounding high Arab culture a newfangled notion of secular literary expression. Even in periods when Jews had no option at all of secular cultural activity, the evidence of what they composed in Hebrew argues that they never ceased to respond to the literary dimension of the Bible, however fervently they saw it in doctrinal or theological terms. The double canonicity of the Song of Songs is a particularly instructive instance of this general phenomenon. As is well known, the Song's reveling in the pleasures of love was elevated to canonical acceptability through allegorical interpretation—in the Jewish treatment, by reading the lover as the Holy One and the beloved as His bride, the Community of Israel. Imaginative energy was lavished on this allegory through the centuries and, far from being an arid scheme, it became deeply moving for countless Jews, as liturgical, mystical, and homiletic texts bear witness. (The classical Kabbalah would have been immeasurably diminished without it.) Judah Halevi (1075?–c. 1141), perhaps the greatest poet of the Spanish period, could use the allegory quite poignantly in some of his liturgical poems by boldly reviving the frank eroticism of the Song in his representation of Israel's relationship with God.

But Hebrew readers, however piously they accepted the allegorical interpretation, could scarcely forget that the Song of Songs was a collection of love poems; and so even in the period before the Andalusian renascence, one finds pointed allusions to the Song in Hebrew epithalamia, poems composed to celebrate the unions of flesh-and-blood brides and grooms. Even the liturgical chanting of the Song had a double justification. The synagogal recitation was fixed for the Sabbath of Passover. Because Passover celebrates the exodus from Egypt, the doctrinal warrant for the linking of the Song with this holiday would be the wilderness phase of the nation's history, which in the allegorical scheme corresponds to the period of honeymoon intimacy between God and Israel His bride (compare the bridal metaphor in Jeremiah 2:2). But Passover is also a spring festival, and the evocation of the beauty of the vernal landscape in the Song of Songs was surely not lost on the framers of the liturgy, even if they were often inclined to obscure the connection between spring and the delights of young love in these poems.

Here are the first five lines of an anonymous alphabetic acrostic composed in Palestine sometime in the Byzantine period and intended for use in the Passover liturgy. The repeated farewell that is bid to the rain is not only a mark of the end of the rainy season in Palestine during the month of April but a formal prelude to the prayer for dew, in-

voked in the alternating refrain, that is inserted in
the Passover service.

Let me utter song as the songbird's season comes,
     and I shall call out in song: go in peace,
       O rain.
On the deeds of my Rock let me look, they are
  sweet in their season,
     and sweetly shall I speak: come in peace,
       O dew.
The rain has gone, the winter's past,
     and all is new-minted in beauty: go in peace,
       O rain.
Mandrakes give off their scent in the lovers'
  garden,
     and cares are gone: come in peace, O dew.
The earth is crowned with grain and wine,
     every creature shouts: go in peace, O rain.[2]

Here, at the heart of the holiday liturgy, the
poetry of nature and love of the Song of Songs
comes to life again in the evocative play of allusions
of the *paytan,* the anonymous liturgical poet. In this
setting of public worship, he duly praises "the deeds
of my Rock," which are not invoked in the biblical Song, but God's wondrous acts are manifested

in these lines in the vernal freshness of nature, the passing of the rainy season, the lovers' garden — in the Song it is both a metaphor for the woman's body and the couple's trysting place. The language of the paytan is a supple interweave of his own formulations with phrases from the Song of Songs, liberated from the vehicle of allegory — "the songbird's season comes," "The rain has gone, the winter's past," "Mandrakes give off their scent." A small but instructive measure of the poet's relation to his biblical source is his deployment of soundplay in the fourth line. In the acrostic scheme, the line begins with daleth, the fourth letter of the Hebrew alphabet; the poet highlights the prominence of the initial consonant by reproducing a lovely pun from the Song and then trumping it. The Hebrew for "mandrakes" is *duda'im,* a supposedly aphrodisiac fruit matched in sound and meaning with *dodim,* "lovers" (this plural form of the noun also means "lovemaking"). To this biblical pun, the poet adds, in the next part of the line, the vanishing of "cares," *deva'im.* This last little move is not one he would have made were he not reading the Song with a careful eye to its poetic craft. A Hebrew poet himself, he observes with great nicety the harmonious orchestration of delicate poetic effects in the Song, and he gives evidence of having in effect asked himself: how can I use this beautiful material, make it part of my own idiom, even go it one better? None of this calls into question the liturgical poet's acceptance of the Song of Songs as a "genuine and inspired book," in all likelihood with the sublimation of human love into theological allegory as the proof of its inspired status. But it was also canonical for him in the same way that Shakespeare was canonical for Keats or Blake for Yeats—as one of the luminous poetic achievements in his language that could both kindle his imagination of the world and suggest to him a set of technical resources.

When secular Hebrew poetry experiences its astounding rebirth in Spain a few centuries later, the range of allusive relation to the biblical texts becomes much broader, with specific instances of allusion often proving to be remarkably subtle, inventive, and sometimes quite startling. Some of the more broad-gauge invocations of biblical models are of a sort familiar in other literatures. Just as the blind Milton could associate his plight, cast among the new Philistines of the Restoration, with that of the blind Samson, Solomon ibn Gabirol (1021–1050s), shunned by many of his fellow Jews for his mystical beliefs and suffering from tuberculosis of the skin, repeatedly identified his painful destiny with that of Job. A writer may read Scripture as a purely doctrinal canon and yet allow himself such personal identifications. Indeed, he may want to give a large theological-historical resonance to his own experience precisely through this sort of identification, as did Samuel Hanagid (993–1056), who as vizier of Granada and commander of its army, saw himself as a second David, and composed two striking victory poems after leading his forces in military triumph, each with 150 lines, the number of Psalms in the canonical collection.

But literature, as every good writer knows, exists in the details, and it is particularly in their imaginative response to the minute details of the Hebrew text of the Bible that the Spanish Hebrew poets register their fine understanding of its literary, and not just religious, canonicity. Here is the opening line of a poem by Hanagid that is part of a cycle of poems on the death of his brother Isaac (a cycle that is one of the great peaks of personal poetry in all medieval literature). The poet has returned to visit his brother's grave the day after the burial: "Alas, I've come back in my spirit's strait, / God be gracious to you, my brother."[3] The second hemistich, as unexceptional as it may seem in translation, reflects an extraordinary condensation of meaning through allusion to the Bible. Even as it perfectly fits a metrical scheme that allows no variations (u - - - u), it is a verbatim quotation of Genesis 43:29, with a single term of familial relation altered. When Benjamin, Joseph's only full brother, is brought down to the Egyptian court by the sons of Leah and the concubines, the man who is vizier of Egypt greets him by saying, "God be gracious to you, my son." Hanagid's substitution of *aḥi,* "my brother," for *beni,* "my son," shows, among other things, how shrewdly he has read Genesis 43 as a great story. Joseph in Egypt beholds the only person in the world he can call "my brother" without emotional or legal reservation, but, still preserving appearances as an Egyptian nobleman, he is careful to address the younger man as "my son." The moment when he will "fall on the neck of Benjamin his brother and weep" (Gen. 45:14) is not yet ripe. Hanagid understands that "my son" is a mask for "my brother," which Joseph longs to pronounce but cannot yet permit himself to utter. The predicament of the medieval poet, whose own political career would surely have encouraged him to identify with the Hebrew lad who became vice regent of Egypt, is painfully the reverse of the biblical figure's quandary: Joseph says "my son" just before he will be reunited with his brother after two decades of separation; Hanagid says "my brother" in the wrenching knowledge that he is now separated from him forever. In the next five lines, he implores his brother to respond to his greeting and then cannot keep himself from imagining the body already beginning to moulder in the grave. Hanagid was, of course, a believing Jew who accepted the inspired status of Scripture (and who was also a recognized authority on rabbinic law), but at moments like this, which abound in his poetry and in that of his contemporaries, he speaks as a person wrestling with his individual human fate who reads in the Bible not law or doctrine but the profound representation of human relationships and of people struggling with the burden of their individual destinies.

The language and imagery of the Bible provided the medieval poets a vehicle for imagining the world, for seeing its beauty, its depth of meaning, sometimes its contradictions and ironies. In many instances, like the one from Hanagid that we have just considered, the relation between the medieval poem and the biblical intertext proves to be one of dialectical complexity. Often, the relation between the two texts is richly consonant, as in the allu-

sion to the creation story near the end of *Hatir-
∂of na'arut,* Judah Halevi's exquisite poem about an
imagined sea voyage. After an awesome night storm
that almost destroys the ship, the sky clears and
the surface of the water gradually returns to tran-
quility:

and the stars are bewildered in the heart of the
    sea
    like exiles banished from their home,
and in their likeness, by their image, they make
    light
    in the heart of the sea, like flames and fires.[4]

The lovely paradox of the stars reflected in the
still undulating water as bewildered exiles banished from their true home sets off a whole train
of associations. The stars recall "the heavens . . .
and all their array" of Genesis 2:1. By implication,
the storm that has just passed is identified with the
primordial "welter and waste" (Genesis 1:2) that
preceded the first act of creation. The starlight reflected in the water thus intimates a renewal of creation. (In the three remaining lines of the poem,
the poet plays with the opposition in Genesis between the waters above and the waters below, di-
vided by a "vault," *raqi'a,* with a linking and mir-

roring between above and below stressed instead of the biblical theme of separation.) The stars in the sky that seem to reproduce themselves in the depths of the sea replicate the act of the Creator who made the "human in our image, by our likeness, to hold sway over the fish of the sea and the fowl of the heavens" (Genesis 1:26).[5] After the storm, the world is knit together again in beautiful harmony, as it was in the first creation. Halevi's use of the allusion demonstrates that reading the two canonicities of the Bible can be entirely simultaneous for the Hebrew poet. To think of creation as it is represented in the first two chapters of Genesis is, necessarily, to think of divine creation, and though this poem is intensely personal, and in its vividness is also a descriptive nature poem, it begins by referring to the poet's obligations to God, and it would be thoroughly misleading to call it a secular poem. And yet, the poet has clearly read Genesis both as the inspired account of how the world came into being and as a complex of suggestive images, virtually a model for the poet's craft. In this way, there is a seamless continuity of poetic artifice between the ornate trope for the night's beauty borrowed from the Arabic tradition that appears in the line before the two we are considering—"the night . . . is like a Negress adorned with golden spangles"—and the image of the stars "in their likeness, by their image" making small flames in the heart of the sea.

There is another, more radical manifestation of intertextuality in medieval and Renaissance poetry in which the words of the biblical texts are willfully wrenched from their original setting and flaunted by the poet in a context that is disparate from, or even antithetical to, the biblical one. There is a dizzying variety of such radical intertextuality through eight centuries of secular Hebrew poetry and rhyming prose. I will cite one brief example, a two-line poem by Judah Halevi, before reflecting on what so bold a use of Scripture might imply about the relation of the poet to the canonical text. The Arabic superscription in the Halevi *diwan*—the manuscript of his collected poems—introduces the poem as follows: "and he spoke [it] in the genre of love poems when he saw one of his friends asleep."

Arise, O my friend, from your slumber,
    sate me when awake with your image.
Should you behold someone kissing your lips in a
    dream,
        it is I who will solve your dreams.

The biblical idiom "solver of dreams" *(poter ḥalomot)* is associated with Joseph, but in this playfully erotic context, solving the riddle of the dream is not an act of interpretation but a kiss given by the speaker to his friend, a fulfillment, that is, of the "prophecy" of the dream. The "slumber" and "image" at the end of the first and second hemistichs are the same word transformed by metathesis *(tenumatekha* turned into *temunatekha)* and a small indication of how Halevi's virtuosity defies translation. But the second hemistich is also a verbatim quotation of the last three Hebrew words of Psalm 17 (only one syllable modified for the sake of the meter). When the Psalmist says, "Sate me [literally, "let me be sated"] when awake with your image," he is of course addressing God. The poetic parallelism in the first half of this verse reads, "I in righteousness shall behold Your face." Halevi is recalling the whole biblical line when he chooses the verb *behold (teḥezeh)* for the friend's erotic dream-vision. The intertext from Psalm 17 may also suggest that the speaker is unable to see his friend's face because of the position in which he is sleeping, which would be a practical motive for urging him to awake. In sum, "when awake," a phrase of rhetorical emphasis with approximately the force of "actually" in Psalms, is entirely literalized in the poem, while the physical matrix of the verb "to be sated" *('esb'a)* is actualized here by the appetitive narrative context of the hoped-for kiss.

What does it say about the Hebrew poet's relation to Scripture that he should feel free to make such audacious and frankly erotic use of a devotional text from the Bible? Let me stress that the radical freedom of allusive play with the Bible manifested in this little poem of Halevi's is thoroughly characteristic of countless love poems, whether homosexual or heterosexual, in the Spanish period, as it is of the bawdy passages of Emmanuel of Rome in the fourteenth century and of a whole spectrum of Hebrew poets of the Italian Renaissance, and not only in instances of erotic verse. There are no grounds to question the fact that Judah Halevi and nearly all the participants in the great medieval and Renaissance tradition of Hebrew literature were religious Jews—not only in their formal commitment to the laws and institutions of rabbinic Judaism but also, in his case and that of a good many others, in possessing a deep sense of piety. Halevi was, after all, a passionate and serious theologian. He surely must have believed that the Book of Psalms, with the rest of Scripture, was the inspired word of God. What allowed him, then, to take this verse from Psalm 17 and flagrantly turn it around from God to man, from epiphany to a kiss? If the canonicity of the Bible were strictly a matter of doctrinal truth (or, as contemporary critics applying *canon* to secular works would say, of ideological conformity), such radical redirecting of biblical language would be unimaginable.

But for Halevi, as for hundreds of other Hebrew poets—and many thousands of Hebrew readers—in the tradition he helped to define, the canonicity of the Bible also inheres in its being the literary repository of the language of the culture. By *language* I mean first, in the fundamental sense, the words and idioms through which it becomes possible to say anything at all. (One must keep constantly in mind that Jews never ceased producing literature in Hebrew, even through the many centuries when it had no vernacular base, and if they also wrote in other languages, Hebrew remained the privileged vehicle of national literature.) In this basically lexical sense, the Bible does not generate allusion in any strict application of the term but rather enables expression. The Bible is also, however, the great compendium of cultural references for its Hebrew readers, who are presumed to have a word-by-word familiarity with it: images, motifs, narrative situations are there to be called up by a writer with the flick of a phrase, and just as in the case of shared cultural references in a purely secular setting, the writer feels free to ride with the semantic sweep of the original text, or to swim against it with athletic vigor, recontextualizing the biblical materials, wittily turning them on their head, even sometimes deconstructing them. The sort of operation T. S. Eliot performs in "The Hollow Men" on a nursery rhyme ("Here We Go Round the Mulberry Bush") in making it, rather startlingly, the expression of a kind of vapid apocalypse ("This is the way the world ends, / This is the way the world ends . . .") is not different in kind from what the Hebrew poets do again and again with the Bible: one could even say that in Jewish societies in which the nursery rhymes were, after all, sung in Judeo-Arabic, Ladino, and Yiddish, the Bible was the Hebrew text everybody educated would immediately know, like a nursery rhyme. As a pious Jew, Halevi no doubt heard in Psalm 17 an authentic anguished cry of the believer for God to rescue him from the arrogant and grant him a glimpse of the divine presence. As a lively member of a living Hebrew literary culture, Halevi seizes the concluding verse of the psalm with manifest delight as matter for inventive transformation: the "beholding" of God's face becomes the friend's beholding of a kiss in his dream, and the longing to be sated with God's image turns into a longing for the image of the friend. From a doctrinal point of view, this is double blasphemy, substituting man for God in the biblical text and man for woman in the expression of passion, but the poet does it without noticeable compunction, for in his sense of the *literary* canonicity of the Bible, considerations of doctrine are suspended.

Such acts of free play with Scripture, it must be said, are carried out in this tradition within a delimited arena. At least some of the poetic genres of the Spanish period, like the love poem, might in fact be thought of precisely as an arena of this sort, a safe space — roughly analogous to the social institution of carnival — in which anything goes with the Bible. The basic difference, I think, between this whole movement of secular Hebrew literature and the one that is launched in Central and Eastern Europe in the wake of the Enlightenment and then Romanticism is that in the more recent movement the second canonicity of the Bible becomes the matrix for the conscious, even programmatic, creation of a secular Hebrew culture. In the medieval and Renaissance tradition, any transvaluing of biblical texts is played out locally, hedged in by the limits of poetic genre. In the formative European phase of modern Hebrew literature (schematically, 1751 to 1917), the transvaluation is global in a double sense: it involves, with the passage of time and for increasing numbers of the writers, an impulse to displace entirely the doctrinal canonicity of the Bible with its literary canonicity; and it is sometimes manifested not merely in playful transformation of biblical texts (this still abounds) but in ideological polemic with biblical values.

Both in poetry and in prose, the age-old sense of the Hebrew Bible as a literary canon, not only a religious one, was what initially made it possible for the new Hebraists to find their way, however awkwardly, into the realm of European literature. The centrally influential poem of the German period of the Haskalah (Hebrew Enlightenment) is Naphtali Hertz Weisel's *Shirei tiferet (Songs of Glory)*, published in segments between 1789 and 1811, a didactic epic on the life of Moses loosely imitative of Klopstock (who produced German epic poetry on biblical themes in hexameter verse). This turgid rhetorical performance is almost unreadable today, but it excited Hebrew imaginations throughout the nineteenth century because it was felt to demonstrate how the literary grandeur of the Hebrew Bible might be the source for new works that could take their place in the high epic tradition of European literature. Two generations later, in Russia, the first Hebrew novel, Avraham Mapu's *Ahavat Tsiyon* (*Love of Zion*, 1853), which is set in the time of Isaiah, in a style that is a florid pastiche of biblical phrases, reflects an analogous aspiration to build on the aesthetic resonances of the Bible and make out of them a new edifice of secular culture in Hebrew. This early step in prose fiction was only a little less stumbling than the ones in epic poetry, but what concerns us here is not the level of artistic success—that would come with a remarkable group of Russian Hebrew writers around the turn of the twentieth century—but rather the nature of the cultural enterprise, the creation of a secular literature enabled by the literary perception of the biblical canon.

Still more instructive in regard to the two orders of authority exerted by the Bible on its Hebrew readers are the polemic engagements with Scripture in a variety of modern Hebrew texts, for they vividly demonstrate how the imaginative power of biblical literature could energize a writer in the very act of his rejecting its ideological values. The two commanding poets of the great efflorescence of Hebrew literature that began in Odessa in the 1890s, Haim Nahman Bialik (1873–1934) and Saul Tchernikhovsky (1875–1943) express this polemic impulse in strikingly different ways. Bialik, the more deeply rooted of the two in traditional Jewish culture, was inclined, as Tchernikhovsky was not, to see his role as Hebrew poet in light of the vocation of the biblical prophet, reading the dedication of the prophet in Isaiah 6 back through Pushkin's recasting of it as a trope for the calling of the poet. But both historical circumstances and the nature of his audience led Bialik more and more to despair of his supposedly prophetic vocation, and thus to transform it radically in a series of daunting poems in which the poet-prophet brings a vision of death or nihilistic hopelessness to his audience. In several ways the most extreme transformation of the prophetic calling is Bialik's awesome long poem on the Kishinev pogrom of 1903, *Be'ir haharegah*, "In the City of Slaughter." Rhetorically, the poet draws on all the prophetic books, but in particular on Ezekiel: the poet-prophet is addressed as "son of man," Ezekiel's idiom, by the voice, presumably God's, that speaks the poem, and is enjoined to "go forth into the city of slaughter" and witness, corpse by mangled corpse, the mayhem perpetrated there. But this God is one who has "declared bankruptcy" *(yaraдti minekhaдai)* in allowing such horrors to happen, and the poem is informed by a corrosive rage against both God and the Jews who cravenly submitted to their attackers. If biblical prophecy is the vehicle for conveying divine wrath to a wayward Israel so that the people can change its course, and thus always implies the urgent engagement of prophet with people, this poem ends with God's commanding the prophet to flee to the rocky wilderness, where he is to "tear [his] soul into ten pieces" and "let [his] heart be consumed by impotent rage." The poetic power of biblical prophecy thunders through this great poem, but in the baleful historical light of the horrors witnessed by the poet, the prophetic idea of divine reward and punishment in history and the biblical prospect of national redemption are scathingly rejected. Later, I shall consider in detail another long poem of Bialik's that makes spectacular use of biblical diction and images and takes off from a biblical story while cultivating a poetic voice and a cosmic vision altogether alien to the literature of the Bible.

In Bialik there is often antagonistic tension with the biblical vehicle he uses because his ideological agenda, prompted by his mentor, Ahad Ha'am, is the perpetuation of classical Jewish values in the modern secular context, a project that in his most probing poetic perceptions sometimes seemed a maddeningly desperate contradiction. (Ahad Ha'am, "One of the People," is the pen name for Asher Ginzberg, 1856–1926, the ideologue of so-called Cultural Zionism, who proposed a synthesis between certain trends of nineteenth-century progressive thought and the legacy of Jewish culture.) Tchernikhovsky, altogether a less "Judaic" poet, is associated with the turn-of-the-century Nietzchean trend in Hebrew writing that aspired to a radical transvaluation of Jewish values. Instead of Bialik's sharp confrontation with biblical assumptions, Tchernikhovsky uses the magic of the Bible's poetic language — which is predominant in many of his strophic poems, in contradistinction to his hexameter idylls — to conjure up what amounts to a counterbiblical world. The implicit theology of Tchernikhovsky's poetry is vitalistic pantheism. His typical move is to inscribe in vivid biblical language at the center of his poems what is proscribed in the Bible — the sun god, Tammuz,

Baal, Ashtoreth, fertility rites, the exultation of
sacred ecstatic dance, the fierce excitement of a
warrior culture. In all this, he was the precursor
of the so-called Canaanite Movement that became
prominent in Hebrew literature in Palestine in the
early 1940s. Here is the sestet of "My Ashtoreth,"
a sonnet written in Russia during the First World
War. (Tchernikhovsky's accentual syllabic prosody
is based on the Ashkenazic or European pronunciation of Hebrew, which gives a penultimate stress
to most words. The music of his poetry, alas, has
vanished when it has been read in the Israeli accent, with its predominant stress on the last syllable.) The speaker, a young woman, is marveling
over a statuette of the fertility goddess Ashtoreth,
which she imagines may have been brought from
Phoenecia in the north by a camel caravan making
its way past Danite — that is, Israelite — marauders:

Wondrous to me, O wondrous, your emerald
    eyes,
        all ivory-wrought, the whole your limbs
            comprise,
And none shall betray how I got you — none.

        A basket of dates for you — I've scooped up
           fine flour,

A lōg of olive oil — to you, in prayer's hour:
  "Lead him, a shining lad, to me bring him
   soon."[6]

In the Hebrew, the only word in these six lines
that is not biblical is "emerald" — but even that postbiblical term is assimilated to a biblical idiomatic
pattern, *'eynayikh 'ismaragdim* recalling the Song
of Song's *'eynayikh yonim* ("your eyes are doves").
There is also a kind of reminiscence of the Song of
Songs, not quite an allusion, in "all ivory-wrought"
(literally: "all of you they have made from ivory"),
as "all of you" *(kulakh)* in the Song punctuates the
ecstatic descriptions of the beloved, and the lover's
loins are said to be fashioned from ivory. But in
contrast to the playful little love poem by Judah
Halevi, Tchernikhovsky's poem does not turn on
any pointed allusion. The sonnet could not have
come into being without his deep experience of the
imaginative power of the Bible in Hebrew, but he
is not ultimately concerned with the Bible as a system of meanings with which to wrestle, verse by
verse. What the Bible presents to him is not doctrinal authority — the first of its two canonicities
scarcely exists for him — but a living world bodied
forth in language, like the world of Homer (whom

Tchernikhovsky translated), or the world of *War and Peace.* The purpose of the poem is to tease out of the shadowy margins of the biblical world into the sunlight of poetic attention what biblical doctrine opposed and suppressed—the fresh pagan (or perhaps, syncretistic) faith of a nubile young woman offering sacrifice and imploring the goddess to send her a lover. The celebration of the aesthetic and of the beauty of the body in the sonnet, and in Tchernikhovsky's poetry as a whole, expresses a counter-value to the dominant value system of the Bible, though this very celebration takes off, instructively, from a whole set of biblical cues. Some of this reflects reading the Bible against itself, as when the poet draws items from the sacrificial lists in Leviticus and uses them for the offering to a fertility goddess. But the intrinsic heterogeneity of the biblical canon is also vital to the poet's undertaking. The fragmentary hints the Bible incorporates of an epic background that was of little interest to the monotheistic writers come to life in the compact vision of a large and exciting Near Eastern horizon evoked in the octave of the sonnet. The celebration of the lovely statuette is predicated on the celebratory love poetry of the Song of Songs, a biblical text which, as we have seen, is exceptional and in a way heterodox. Most pervasively, the implicit feeling of so many of the biblical writers in different genres and books for the expressive loveliness of their Hebrew medium makes possible Tchernikhovsky's own aestheticizing of the biblical world.

Tchernikhovsky's poetic enterprise is, I think, one of those instances of the extreme case that illuminates an underlying dynamic of the typical. His brave attempt to help forge a secular, or at any rate, nonmonotheistic cultural identity in Hebrew has encountered serious challenges in the half-century since his death. This is not the place to speculate as to whether Jewish secularism, or Jewish cultural nationalism, still has a future. What is pertinent to our concerns here is the sheer power of the Bible's second canonicity that created the possibility of the cultural alternative articulated in Tchernikhovsky's poetry. If the formation of the biblical canon two millennia ago reflected the crystallization of a religious ideology, there were also, as is patently true in secular canons, impulses that transcended ideology or even subverted it, which went into the making of the canon. For Hebrew readers through the ages, these impulses were not merely archaeological traces of vanished intentionalities but palpable presences in the texts. Through them creative imaginations have been repeatedly sparked, and some of the most surprising cultural blossoms have sprung from the rich old soil of the Bible. If the canon, in this supposedly exemplary case, turns out to be more dynamic and multifaceted than its doctrinal function would require, we should not be surprised to discover that secular canons similarly prove to be bustling junctions of contradictory aims and values, and not, as many of the new critics of the canon claim, vehicles for the enforcement of ideological conformity.

Postbiblical Hebrew literature, as I have tried to show, and as we shall have occasion to see again in a closer look at Bialik, is in one respect a special case because of the compelling linguistic continuity it exhibits with the ancient canonical texts. Nevertheless, the imaginative response to the Bible of writers in a wide variety of languages bears witness to a power of canonicity that is not limited to doctrine or strictly contingent on belief in the inspired character of the texts invoked. Modern literature is not unique in this regard; but, in its very impulse to question received ideas, to shake up old forms, conventions, and values, it lays bare a partly submerged impulse in the relation of writers at all times to the biblical canon and in certain respects to the literary canon as well. In what follows, I shall consider three exemplary modern instances. The fiction of Franz Kafka will be a useful point of departure. In his formal and theological iconoclasm, he is often thought of as the paradigmatic modernist, yet his fascination with the Bible also reflects a surprising spiritual kinship with the tradition, for all the peculiar spin he puts on biblical texts. Bialik then presents an instructive paradox as a poet steeped in the Bible, writing vigorously in the Bible's own language, articulating a radical alternative to the Bible's world of values that would scarcely have occurred to Kafka, the supposed iconoclast. Finally, we shall consider the case of Joyce's *Ulysses*, that central masterwork of modernist fiction, in which there is neither interpretive wrestling with the Bible, as in Kafka, nor rebellion against it, as in Bialik, but through the very act of intricately coordinating Scripture with Homer, a shifting of the authority of the Bible to new grounds.

2
Franz Kafka
Wrenching Scripture

At first thought, it would seem that Kafka's relation to the Bible is strictly analogous to his relation to Judaism: a concern that urgently engaged him in his private writings and that he rigorously excluded from his fiction. The analogy, however, does not entirely hold, for the first of his three novels, as I shall try to show, invokes an elaborate network of conflated allusions to Genesis and Exodus, which are thematically imperative, for all their transmogrification in a fantasized American setting. This use of biblical materials in a modern setting, at once playful and thematically serious, reflects both the afterlife of authority and the altered standing of the Bible in modernist writing.

Kafka's effort to make something for his inner life of Jewish tradition was first catalyzed, as is

well known, by the visit to Prague of a Yiddish the-
atrical group in 1911 (just a few months after he
began work on his American novel). It is thus a
preoccupation of the last dozen years of his brief
life. These are also, of course, the years when he
produced his most compelling fiction. During this
period, he began to read about Jewish history, Yiddish literature, Hasidism, and related topics in German, and from 1917 onward he devoted some of
his already failing energies to learning Hebrew. He
achieved sufficient knowledge of the language to
work his way arduously, with the help of a dictionary, through a recent Hebrew novel by Y. H.
Brenner, to read passages in the Hebrew Bible,
and to look into Rashi's commentary on the Pen-
tateuch. Toward the end, he made some attempt to
study the Talmud as well. In any event, the com-
ponent of Jewish tradition that would have been
most directly accessible to his intense scrutiny was
its founding text, the Bible, chiefly read by him, of
course, in Luther's translation.

There is something almost uncanny about
Kafka as a reader of the Bible. Midrash, Talmud,
and Kabbalah were certainly not part of his formative cultural experience, and even his late acquain-
tance with them was rather marginal. Yet the way

he read the Bible reflected a spiritual kinship with these classical vehicles of Jewish exegesis. Such kinship, which may look like a kind of spontaneous intellectual atavism, defies any simple causal explanation. My guess is that it has a good deal to do with Kafka's habitual concentration on the idea of revelation, and on the notion of the Law that in the Jewish view is the principal consequence of revelation for human praxis. That is to say, if you begin with the working assumption that this particular text, which as a canonical text is compact, enigmatic, and charged with a sense of authority, may be divinely revealed, you then proceed to exert terrific interpretive pressure on the text in order to unlock the truth, or multiple truths, it holds for you. Stating the case in this way, I do not presume to know very much about Kafka's actual beliefs. The evidence suggests that he was prone to radical skepticism, but it is equally clear that he found the hypothesis of Scripture as revealed truth alluring, and that he generally adopted that hypothesis in his practice as a reader of the Bible. One might think of it as a continuing thought experiment that Kafka undertook, a thought experiment that both afforded an expression to his theological searching and nourished his imaginative work as a writer of fiction.

Franz Kafka

[65]

Kafka is famously a disruptive modernist in regard to both his handling of literary form and his sense of the world, and so it is hardly surprising that his treatment of Scripture should be paradoxical—at once traditional and iconoclastic. The traditionalism is manifested in the pitch of spiritual tension and acuteness with which he scrutinizes the canonical text, in the midrashic adroitness with which he fleshes out the meanings of the text and endows its relevance to him with narrative palpability. The iconoclasm is reflected in his propensity to spin the text around one hundred and eighty degrees, to wrest from it ideas and values antithetical to its own ostensible intentions, and certainly antithetical to the interpretive consensus of tradition. If Kafka is a midrashic reader of Scripture, what he often proposes is a heretical midrash. It is this trait that led Gershom Scholem, in the last of his "Ten Ahistorical Theses on the Kabbalah," to compare Kafka's reflections on the Garden of Eden with those of an eighteenth-century radical antinomian, a follower of Jacob Frank, and to conclude that "Kafka gave expression to the borderline between religion and nihilism, and so his writings possess . . . in the eyes of certain readers of our era [Scholem is clearly thinking of himself and kindred spirits], something of the rigorous light of canon-icity."[1]

Before considering in detail the boldness and verve with which Kafka integrated biblical motifs into his American novel, let us look at the sort of radical midrash he constructed on one biblical text. It was Genesis, the book of origins, that engaged him more than any other in the biblical canon, and he was especially drawn to three topics—the first paradise, Abraham the first father, and the Tower of Babel. On the Tower of Babel he wrote four different midrashic reflections. There were, I think, two different features of that very brief and resonant story which spoke to his imagination. One was the human aspiration it recorded to reach up to the realm of the divine, to transgress eternally fixed boundaries: "Come, let us build us a city and a tower with its top in the heavens," the builders of Babel proclaim. The other aspect of the Tower of Babel that may have addressed a deep concern in Kafka, though he gave it no explicit expression in his readings, was its account of the origins of linguistic division. The biblical notion of the multiplicity of languages as a curse, a loss of primordial unity, surely would have haunted him, troubled as he sometimes professed to be (whatever the actual facts of the matter) that German was not really his language, a language he perfected in his own idiosyncratic way in predominantly Czech Prague, while often thinking about Yiddish antecedents and then struggling to acquire Hebrew.

Kafka's most quizzical reflection on the Tower, actuated by the same impulse to spiritual paradox that informs his musings on the Garden of Eden, is this brief sentence: "If it had been possible to build the Tower of Babel without ascending it, the work would have been permitted."[2] This paradox takes for granted, as a traditional reading would, the immutable authority of the biblical tale: its canonicity is not called into question. But it also reads the biblical text against the grain, teasing out of it an idea that contradicts the explicit condemnation in Genesis of the effort of the builders as an act of overweening presumption. This reader of the Bible sees the vision of a human edifice touching the heavens as a compelling aspiration, man in a perhaps Nietzchean fashion reaching beyond his own limits, striving to become more than himself. If the idea of human self-transcendence could have been nurtured without the transgressive act of its implementation, the Tower would have been no sin. Thus the imperative force of Scripture is left in place while the interpreter's twist of perspective on the biblical tale opens up a horizon of values that the biblical writer is not likely to have envisaged.

A second brief variation on the Tower story, entirely in dialogue, vividly etches that responsiveness to "the comic aspects of Jewish theology" which Walter Benjamin, in a late letter to Scholem, identified as one of Kafka's defining features.[3] "What are you building?" an anonymous questioner calls out. To which the person interrogated responds: "I want to dig a passage. Some progress must be made. My station up there is too high. We are digging the pit of Babel" (p. 35, translation modified). This droll exchange is, of course, a precise rotation of the biblical story from up to down, but it also accords a certain respect to the biblical text, seeking, as the classical midrash does, to bridge the yawning gap between the interpreter and the text. The heroic, or presumptuous, stretch for transcendence of the builders of the Tower, admired in the previously cited text, is simply beyond the imaginative reach of this postheroic personage, who instead, like the mole of Kafka's story, burrows into a hole in the ground. (The German word translated as "pit," *Schacht,* could also mean "mine shaft.") The idea, it should be stressed, of a mine shaft of Babel is funny exactly in Benjamin's theological sense, rather than silly. The story in Genesis 11 reflects the powerful yearning of the human creature to achieve impossibly great things. Kafka's reversal of the canonical tale sustains the perception of that yearning, assumes it as an essential trait of man, yet tries to imagine how the age-old impulse would play out in a fallen reality, where man is scared of the heights, content to push forward his concerted projects in the shelter of the underground, with transcendence turned into a negative or perhaps a parody of the original. The textual image of the canonical is refracted in a fun-house mirror, yet it continues to challenge the life of the interpreter.

Of Kafka's two somewhat longer reflections on the Tower, the one that comes closer to a midrashic model of reading Scripture is the piece that his English editors have entitled "The City Coat of Arms" (*Parables and Paradoxes*, pp. 37, 39). The opening lines share with the Midrash an impulse to flesh out the spare biblical tale and to make it intelligible in more or less contemporary terms: "At first all the arrangements for building the Tower of Babel were characterized by fairly good order; indeed the order was perhaps too perfect, too much thought was taken for guides, interpreters, accommodation for the workmen, and roads of communication, as if there were centuries before one to do the work in." A single word slipped into this contemporary realization of Genesis 11 drastically shifts the grounds of the canonical story — *Dolmetscher,* "interpreters," that is, translators. The division of languages is no longer a consequence of human presumption, a divinely inflicted punishment, but a given of the human condition, which itself will be adduced to explain the failure of the Tower. First, the building does not go forward because of collective procrastination: through the constant progress — *Fortschritt,* the same goal to which the digger of the Pit of Babel is committed — of technology, in a century or two the work will be completed far more swiftly and more soundly, so why build the Tower now? "Such thoughts," the narrator observes, "paralyzed people's powers, and so they troubled less about the tower than the construction of a city for the workmen." The building of the city, exploiting the very advances in technology on which the builders had banked, becomes a source of conflict, as each ethnic or national group *(Landsmannschaft),* fighting for the best quarters, violently clashes with the others.

Franz Kafka

[71]

In one crucial respect, this reading radically reverses Genesis. Biblical "after" turns into Kafkan "before"—divisiveness is not the consequence of the aborted attempt to build the Tower but the very cause of its abortion, and a naturalistic explanation replaces the supernatural one in which God's intervention (divine descent symmetrically answering human ascent) confounds the builders. But for all this shifting of grounds, Kafka's reading retains a firm grip on the thematic core of the biblical story. "The essential thing in the whole undertaking is the idea of building a Tower that will reach the heaven" (translation modified). Kafka steadily sees that the Babel story is an urgent parable of the allure for the human spirit of overreaching aspiration: "The idea, once seized in its magnitude, can never vanish again; so long as there are men, there will also be the powerful desire to complete the building" (translation modified). This ringing declaration is qualified by a dialectical countermove toward the end of the parable: the would-be builders, trapped in the internecine strife of the city, begin to think that the building of a tower to the heavens is actually pointless. Here at its conclusion, Kafka's reading embraces a second urgent theme of the original biblical story—its antiurbanism. The ancient Hebrew writer, from his perspective in a little nation of pastoralists and agriculturalists, viewed the urban concentration of power, technology, and population of the great surrounding empires as an expression of humankind's morally dangerous grandiosity. Kafka, writing in an urban and technological environment three millennia removed from the setting of Genesis 11, shares this fundamental perception of the biblical text. Indeed, he amplifies its resonance by concluding his reflection on an apocalyptic note: the intolerable conflicts of urban existence engender a longing for release through destruction, "for a prophesied day when the city would be destroyed by five successive blows from a gigantic fist." (The image of the menacing clenched fist, no doubt psychologically derived from the looming power of the paternal body, is quintessential Kafka.) In this fashion the biblical Babel, upon which modern Prague or any counterpart elsewhere in Europe has been superimposed, also becomes a medieval city that "has a closed fist on its coat of arms." The paradoxical effect is that the authority of the canonical text, its universal relevance, is confirmed even as it is drastically revised.

There is no single, consistent relation to Scripture in Kafka but rather a shifting variety of takes on the biblical text, the one constant being the fact that the Bible grips his imagination, however he twists and turns it. In "The Great Wall and the Tower of Babel" (*Parables and Paradoxes*, pp. 25, 27), he sets the biblical tale in a broad web of scholarly conjecture that sounds more like an anticipation of Borges than a reminiscence of the Midrash. Here, in contrast to the collective voice of the Midrash, we have a first-person narrator or rather, conjecturor. ("I say this because in the early days of building a scholar wrote a book in which he drew the comparison [between the Tower and other construction projects] in the most exhaustive way.") The canonical story retains a certain imperative power, but that power is now highly mediated: the story is a text in a vast library, the point of departure in a universe of exegesis (which is the Kafka universe par excellence), where inferences are drawn, documents and other proofs cited, arguments and counterarguments proposed. In this universe, one of the scholars cited makes the daring proposal "that the Great Wall alone would provide for the first time in the history of mankind a secure foundation for a new Tower of Babel." The first-person conjecturor, however, is bothered by the fact that the Great Wall of China is very far from

Franz Kafka
[74]

forming a complete circle and so could scarcely serve as the foundation for a tower. This perception leads him to the conclusion that the joining of the two monumental building enterprises must be meant only in "a spiritual sense" and that no actual tower need be built. At the end, he passes from the wild multiplicity of scholarly projects to the violent divisiveness of the human spirit that subverts all grandiose undertakings: "Human nature, essentially changeable, unstable as dust, can endure no restraint; if it binds itself it soon begins to tear madly at its bonds, until it rends everything asunder to all points of the compass, the wall, the bonds, and its very self" (translation modified). Again, Babel turns into apocalypse.

This somber view of human nature picks up an emphasis from Genesis, implicit in the Tower story and explicit in the story of the Flood when God declares, "the divisings of the human heart are evil from youth." The odd turn that Kafka gives to the canonical tale, what may chiefly make it seem an anticipation of Borges, is the conflation of the Tower of Babel in the Mesopotamian Valley of Shinar with the Great Wall of China. Even as Kafka's lavishing of exegetical speculation confirms the authority of the biblical text — the measure of the canonical is that the interpreter assumes truth must be derived from the text through the labor of interpretation — biblical canonicity is also quietly compromised because its claim to be the exclusive source of truth is tacitly set aside. A canon in the strict sense is what Moshe Halbertal calls a "sealed text."[4] "Turn it and turn it," as Ben Bag-Bag says in the Mishnaic *Teachings of the Fathers,* "For everything is in it." The universalism of Kafka's perspective, on the other hand, in which the Great Wall and the Tower of Babel may be variants of the same idea, or in which one is necessary to make sense of the other, suggests that the biblical text and the biblical history must be open to other texts and other histories, that Scripture is not the ultimate source of truth but one cultural instance among many of the truths of the human predicament. Kafka's interest in Chinese lore, in the Chinese idea of wisdom (Walter Benjamin has a similar interest), is in one sense strictly coordinate with his interest in the Hebrew Bible. What attracts him is less a definite canon than the phenomenon of canonicity, the allure of the compact, enigmatic tale steeped in tradition that is a constant challenge to exegesis. Indeed, Kafka anticipates or perhaps actually inspires his great admirer Gershom Scholem in seeing endless interpretability rather than absolute truth as the principal criterion of the canonical. Thus the dynamic of the canonical is retained, but its authority is compromised.

This double relation to the canonicity of the Bible, at once an imaginative allegiance to its compelling address to the reader and a readiness to open it to unfamiliar horizons, is reflected in Kafka's fantastic fusion of Genesis and Exodus with a contemporary New York and Oklahoma in the novel he provisionally called *The Man Who Disappeared* and that his literary executor Max Brod entitled *Amerika*.

As if to offer a clue to the biblical background of the novel, Kafka makes sure to include among the few items mentioned that are packed in Karl Rossmann's suitcase a pocket edition of the Bible (no doubt, in Luther's translation). The Bible lies at the bottom of the suitcase next to the photograph of Karl's parents that so mesmerizes him. It is thus associated by contiguity with parental authority— in the person of the father, as we would expect in Kafka, a menacing, violent authority. Karl turns over the pages of the Bible without actually reading, then fixes his gaze on the image of his father, standing with clenched fist—like the fist in "The

City's Coat of Arms"—behind his mother, whose mouth seems to him twisted in pain. The pocket Bible, leafed through as a kind of talisman but left unread, is a token of dramatic irony, for Karl remains oblivious to the contents of the text he holds while the alert reader will have been aware from the first page of the novel that this very text provides much of the thematic definition of Karl's story.[5]

When Karl Rossmann's ship sails into New York harbor in the first paragraph of the novel, a sudden burst of sunlight reveals to him what any new arrival around 1910 would have noticed—the looming figure of the Statue of Liberty. This Statue of Liberty, however, formally announcing at the very beginning that actual America is to be reconfigured as psychologically resonant fantasy, raises on high something other than a torch: "The arm with the sword rose up as if newly stretched aloft, and round the figure blew the free winds."[6] The Freudian edge of the unexpected sword cuts an obvious swath through Karl's story. The three sexually impelled women Karl encounters in the course of the novel all threaten him: Johanna Brummer (her last name means "grumbler"), the hulking servant girl back in Prague, rapes him; young Clara Pollunder uses jujitsu to fling him around like a rag doll; and the corpulent Brunelda crushes him with the overwhelming abundance of her flesh. It is hardly surprising, then, that the first figure of a woman in the novel should be brandishing a phallic sword, neatly assumed by the narrator to be her well-known accoutrement ("the arm with the sword"). But this sword also has a biblical provenance. America offers the possibility of being a new Eden for Karl Rossmann—in one of the novel's two Dickensian intertexts, *Martin Chuzzlewit,* the phony real estate located in swampland is called Eden—and at the gates of Eden in Genesis God sets fearsome cherubim and "the flame of the whirling sword to guard the way to the tree of life." The biblical image at the beginning, in nice accord with subsequent uses of the Bible in the novel, is an aggressive oxymoron: Karl has been banished from his father's house, but the indications of the harsh paternal regime suggest it was no Eden; in turn, his moment of entry into the Eden of the New World invokes a reminiscence of the primordial banishment. (This allusion to the Garden story, together with its unsettling ambiguities, has also been noted by John Hollander, who aptly observes that the sword-wielding statue "implicitly cancels and replaces the figure of a guardian angel . . . assigned to

Franz Kafka
[79]

seal up the eastern gate of lost, emptied Eden."[7])
This fusion of contradictory biblical allusions is an
essential reflection of Kafka's location in existence
—forever a creature in-between, wandering in the
liminal zone of the Wilderness, equally excluded
from the Eden of family origins and from the Promised Land of marriage, Zionism, and spiritual fulfillment.[8] The biblical narrative tells a linear story of
banishment from a particular place, eventual wan-
derings, and entering into another particular place.
In Kafka's conflation of biblical places and themes,
the linearity is dissolved, and we cannot be sure
whether the hero is coming or going.

Karl's ill-fated sojourn in the fabulous New
York apartment of his rich and powerful American
uncle becomes the stage for still another banishment that harks back to the scriptural one. Uncle
Jacob showers kindnesses on Karl, promises him a
brilliant future, but also confronts him with seemingly capricious prohibitions. Karl's first temptation is the excitingly intricate American writing
desk with its combinations and permutations of
shifting drawers and compartments. These are con-
trolled by a delicate mechanism called a regulator, which Karl's uncle repeatedly warns him not to
touch, lest he put it out of order. "It was not hard

to guess that these remarks were merely pretexts, though on the other hand it would have been quite easy to lock the regulator and yet Uncle Jacob refrained from doing so" (p. 42). The analogy with the divine prohibition in Genesis against eating from the tree of knowledge of good and evil is piquant because of its very transposition into the distinctively Kafkan realm of modern gadgetry. Karl manages to resist this temptation, but, like the first humans in the Garden, he continues to find himself surrounded by interdictions he scarcely knows of and cannot fathom. When he takes the seemingly innocuous step of accepting a dinner invitation outside New York from his uncle's business associate, Mr. Pollunder, he is given, that very night at midnight, a peremptory letter from Uncle Jacob dismissing him forever from his presence for this act of betrayal. The echo of the first banishment is underscored when Karl then promptly leaves the Pollunder estate, making his way "out of the garden" amidst the barking of angry dogs into an unfamiliar and perhaps unfriendly world (p. 98).

If Uncle Jacob plays the role of God in the Garden story, he is also aligned with his biblical namesake. Jacob is, after all, Joseph's father, and, as we shall see, Karl Rossmann is very much a

Joseph figure, not merely in relation to this surrogate father. When Karl first notices on board the ship the man he does not yet realize is his uncle, Jacob "was in civilian clothes and carried a thin bamboo cane which, as both his hands were resting on his hip, also stood out like a sword" (p. 13). The psychoanalytically inclined will immediately connect the swordlike cane with the weapon held on high by the Statue of Liberty, but the cane, which will be mentioned several times more, also has a biblical source: Jacob, recalling his arduous journeyings, tells God, "For with my staff I crossed this Jordan; and now I have become two camps." That trajectory from poverty through adversity to great wealth is shared by Uncle Jacob in the novel, who also participates in an archetype of modern European folklore, *mon oncle d'Amérique,* the rich uncle from America fantasized as the providential force in the life of a struggling nephew in the Old World.

Karl on his part would like to cut a Joseph figure in the new land to which he has been abruptly shipped off by his family. He is sixteen upon his arrival, but later the Manageress at the hotel where he is employed will take him for seventeen — exactly Joseph's age when he is sold down into Egypt. He nurtures visions of working his way to the top in the New World, achieving a ringing success, vindicating himself in the eyes of the parents who rejected him. The biblical story of Joseph, one should keep in mind, is the great rags-to-riches story in Scripture, the tale of a brilliant career from abject beginnings that corresponds to a familiar plot in the nineteenth-century novel. In the event, Karl's story will correspond most of all to the moments of humiliation and defeat in the Joseph story. He is subjected to three different versions of Genesis 39, the tale of Joseph and Potiphar's wife. In Genesis, of course, Joseph manages to resist the sexual assault of the older concupiscent woman, leaving his garment in her grasping hand and fleeing naked, to be thrown into prison on the accusation of attempted rape. Kafka's more feeble protagonist is locked in the bedroom by the sex-starved Johanna and helplessly succumbs to her as she "pressed her naked belly against his body, felt with her hand between his legs, so disgustingly that his head and neck started up from the pillows, then thrust her body several times against him" (p. 29). Although it seems to him "as if she were a part of himself," this is by no means the becoming "one flesh" of Genesis 2: he is left with "a terrible neediness" *(Hilfsbedürftig-keit)* and with a sense that almost nothing has really happened to him. There is a reprise of this scene, and of the biblical one, in his nocturnal tussling with Clara: as she tosses him around with great gusto, an undercurrent of sexual invitation is visible in the wave of physical assault, though of course the intimidated Karl will not respond. The previous encounter with a latter-day Lady Potiphar led directly to Karl's disgrace and banishment. That banishment in turn takes him in the New World to a fate of imprisonment, like Joseph in Genesis 39. When he is dismissed from his post as elevator boy at the Hotel Occidental, the Head Porter actually threatens him with imprisonment. Then, in the claustral apartment of Robinson and Delamarche, squeezed against the railing by the copious flesh of Brunelda, who in her overripe sexuality is the novel's third avatar of Potiphar's wife, "he was literally a prisoner" (p. 254).

Imprisonment as threatened fate and metaphor is a central focus of what I would call the spatial thematics of the novel, which moves along a path of progressive constriction—Karl is constantly getting squeezed, crowded, hemmed in—until the final reversal with its liberation into vast spaciousness in the Nature Theatre of Oklahoma. Joseph's Egyptian prison cell in Genesis is conceived here as an adumbration of the early chapters of Exodus, in which all Egypt, "the house of bondage," becomes a prison for the Hebrew people. The boldest paradox in the play with biblical materials in Kafka's novel is that America, alternately the New Eden and the Promised Land, proves to be a modern manifestation of the Egyptian house of bondage.

This correspondence with Exodus is more than one interpreter's fanciful analogy, for Kafka makes a point of giving the town where Karl goes to work the most un-American name Rameses, which is of course one of the two store-cities that the Hebrew slaves were forced to build for Pharaoh. Compulsive, incessant work is in general a topic that preoccupies Kafka. Indeed, it is a theme he attaches to the building of the Tower of Babel. Most prominently in *The Castle*, he offers a series of memorable representations of the frantic whirl of activity, the restless shuffling of dossiers and documents and memoranda, of bureaucratic labor. It is chiefly in *Amerika*, however, that he turns work into a species of enslavement. Therese, Karl's fellow employee at the Hotel Occidental, by way of introducing him to the regimen there, explains that she "wasn't equal to the heavy work. They expect a lot from you here." When she goes on to report how she literally collapsed under the strain, Karl, just having observed an elevator boy asleep on his feet, remarks, "The work here must really be tiring" (p. 140). This is the moment when he goes on to ask the name of the town and is told that it is Rameses. There are no literal pharaonic taskmasters with whips at the Hotel Occidental, but we are repeatedly made aware of the gargantuan proportions of the enterprise — thirty-one elevators and an incessant flow of passengers managed by boys standing through twelve-hour shifts — as we are reminded of "the stupendous hierarchy of the hotel staff" (p. 165). And when Karl, inadvertently and quite helplessly, ends up transgressing the strict code that governs the behavior of the hotel labor force, he is confronted by a Head Waiter and a Head Porter as harsh and vindictive as any ancient taskmaster, and is threatened, as we have noted, with imprisonment.

Therese, who is an immigrant from Pomerania and thus, like Karl, a "Hebrew" worker displaced from her homeland to this latter-day house of bondage, tells him the sad story of her mother's accidental death in the new land — a pile of bricks with a heavy plank at a building site came tumbling down on her. The bricks recall the huge quantities of bricks the Israelites were compelled to make for Pharaoh's construction projects, and the burial by bricks might conceivably suggest the midrash in which the Hebrew slaves are forced to bury their infants among the bricks in the walls of the pyramids. (Kafka, with his distinctive eye for the farcical and bizarre, turns the death into a kind of burlesque rape by the building materials, as Therese describes her mother "lying there in her checkered skirt, which had come all the way from Pomerania, her legs thrown wide, almost covered by the rough plank atop of her" [p. 157].) The other biblical story in which bricklaying is prominent is of course the Tower of Babel. Given Kafka's fascination with the idea of reaching for the heavens in that project, he may be intimating that when humankind's fever of labor lacks a horizon of transcendence, as in biblical Egypt and in his version of modern America, it turns into sheer enslavement.

Karl, expelled in disgrace from the Hotel Occidental, is immediately yanked into the bizarre ménage of Delamarche, Robinson, and Brunelda. He quickly realizes that this new situation is a smaller-scale version, more claustrally restricting, of the bondage he experienced at the hotel: "So far as I can tell from your account of it," he remarks to Robinson, "and from what I have seen myself, this isn't service here, it's slavery. Nobody could endure it" (p. 242). In this penultimate episode of the novel, the Exodus theme of enslavement fuses with the Joseph-story theme of imprisonment. The tiny apartment with its locked door is literally a prison for Karl, and within that prison, the imposing body of the sexually demanding woman becomes a second prison as Brunelda crushes Karl against the railing of the balcony: "He flinched in an involuntary but unsuccessful attempt to escape from the pressure of her body" (p. 248). Kafka's novel thus describes an ingenious interpretive loop around the biblical story of Joseph: in place of the prison to which Joseph is condemned for an alleged sexual crime (as Karl has been sent off to what proves to be the prison house of America for a supposed sexual transgression), the physical presence of the aggressive woman itself becomes the ultimate prison.

How can he get out? It was surely Kafka's difficulty in imagining this necessary extrication that led to the incompletion of the novel. At the end of the Brunelda episode, Karl goes to sleep dreaming once again of how, when he escapes, he will make his way through assiduous effort up the rungs of the

American hierarchy. The last, ominous image of the chapter, however, is of the imperious Brunelda tossing and turning in her sleep. In the concluding fragment, "The Nature Theatre of Oklahoma," across the hiatus of the narrative transition that Kafka was unable to imagine, we have moved from Exodus 1–5 to Exodus 12–15, from the tale of oppressive enslavement to the story of liberation. The placard that invites all comers to join the great theater urges them to "hurry, so that you get there before midnight" (p. 273). The hasty nocturnal departure gestures toward the flight of the Israelites from Egypt in the middle of the night, a departure so precipitous that they had no time to let their dough rise. The blaring of trumpets Karl hears is the counterpart to the blast of ram's horns that was the signal for the Israelites in the wilderness to begin their march. The very stress on music—specifically trumpets and drums, indifferently played—may recall the Exodus song of triumph at the Sea of Reeds, with Miriam dancing to the beat of a timbrel. The ragtag constitution of the crowd of volunteers—"What destitute, disreputable characters were here assembled . . . !" (p. 296)—who flock to the Nature Theatre alludes to the "mixed multitude" who join the Israelites in their flight from Egypt. The image of a man and wife with a small child in a baby carriage on which Karl focuses harks back to Moses' "With our children and our old people we will go."

The Oklahoma fragment breaks off, appropriately enough, with an evocation of the crowded train rushing westward through a vast landscape teeming with variety and pulsing with energy: "narrow, dark, jagged valleys opened out and one tried to follow with a finger the direction in which they lost themselves; broad mountain streams appeared, rushing in great waves down to the hilly lower ground and driving with them a thousand foaming wavelets" (p. 298, translation modified). In terms of what I have called the spatial thematics of the novel, the Oklahoma Theatre is clearly conceived as an opening up to unlimited horizons after all the visions of claustral constriction. The wilderness, or at any rate the glimpse of it we are vouchsafed at the end of the concluding fragment, modulates into the Promised Land itself. Given the fact, moreover, that many of the recruits for the theater have been dressed up as angels, it also incorporates an intimation, vaguely farcical as one would expect in Kafka, of a return to paradise, a final circumvention of the sword-wielding angel whose avatar stood at the gates of Eden in the first paragraph of the novel. Although Kafka did not, after all, work out this thematic conclusion, the idea he began to sketch was that acting, playing, music, and art would provide the alternative to the world of futile, grinding labor in which the protagonist had been trapped. Another parallel from Dickens that suggests itself sheds light on Kafka's intention even if he was not actually familiar with this particular novel: in *Hard Times*, the escape from the modern realm of crushing industrial labor and the equally crushing process of education founded on the principles of utilitarianism is the circus, where fancy — that is, imagination — reigns and where work becomes play.

By now I hope it has become clear that Kafka has fashioned in his biblical novel a rather curious and ingenious amalgam of scriptural materials — beginning with the banishment from Eden, conflating the story of Jacob and Joseph with the account of the enslavement in Egypt and the liberation from bondage in Exodus, and integrating all these biblical motifs into several conventional patterns of the nineteenth-century novel, from bildungsroman to picaresque, projected onto the landscape of a fantastically transformed America. I do not necessarily presume a priority of the biblical scheme in his own creative process. He clearly had a number of models in mind, from the generic one of the bildungsroman to the psychoautobiographical plot of expulsion from the family by a punitive father, a plot that he variously traced in such stories as "The Metamorphosis" and "The Judgment," as well as in "Letter to his Father." Nevertheless, the importance of the Bible to his imaginative project deserves far more attention than it has received.

The resourcefulness and wit with which biblical materials have been deployed reflect a certain characteristically modernist exuberance in the use and transmutation of traditional materials—akin, for example, to Chagall's exuberant transmogrification of motifs taken from Yiddish folklore in his great panoramic mural for the Moscow Yiddish Art Theater.[9] The imaginative freedom, however, with which Kafka alludes to the Bible does not mean that the intention or effect of his work is explicitly to subvert the authority of Scripture. A brief comparison with the use of the Joseph story in a more traditional novelist may help us place Kafka's relation to the Bible in the evolution of literary history against a background of theology. Fielding's *Joseph Andrews* (1743) also follows the fortunes of an innocent young male protagonist who is the repeated object of sexual assault by lustful older women. The novel includes two hilarious replays of Genesis 39, in which the lubricious Lady Booby assumes the role of Potiphar's wife, futilely trying to draw Joseph into bed with her. After her second failure, she has him expelled from her household, where he has been working as a servant, and he is then thrust into a picaresque series of mishaps and adventures on the road before his final triumph. As in *Amerika,* one story from Genesis is yoked with others—Joseph's pastor and comic mentor, Abraham Adams, evokes both Abraham the first father and the innocence of the first man in the Garden. Here, too, the biblical materials are conjoined with European literary conventions: the plot of mistaken identities and ultimately happy coincidence harks back to Hellenistic romance; the self-ironic narrator ostentatiously presents his narrative as a comic epic; and elements of the picaresque are evident as well.

Fielding shares, then, with Kafka a spirit of playful inventiveness in his redeployment of biblical motifs in a contemporary setting. The chief difference is that the eighteenth-century writer confidently assumes the Bible as a timeless source of moral authority, almost a practical guide for skirting the moral pitfalls of everyday life, accessible to anyone who reads it with common sense. He is bolstered in this assumption, as the eminent Fielding scholar Martin Battestin has shown, by a stockpile of set moral values attached to the figures of Joseph and Abraham in the Latitudinarian sermons of his era.[10] Kafka's use of the Bible is quirkier, less predictable. The Bible as he reads it abounds in paradoxes, which he on his part compounds by imposing an exegesis that is itself often highly paradoxical: the promised land can become the site of Egyptian bondage; the pyramids are touched by the shadow of the Tower of Babel, behind which may loom the distant outline of the Great Wall of China. The paradoxical reading of the Bible, of course, is not at all a modern invention. It flourished especially in the heavily charged climate of Jewish mysticism, and Scholem's argument for an affinity between Kafka and the Kabbalah is pertinent precisely in this regard. What must be added is that Kafka shares the confidence neither of Fielding the commonsense Protestant believer nor of the Jewish mystics in the Bible as a faithful map of the moral life. In his treatment of the Joseph story, virtue does not prevail. The young man is physically overwhelmed by the woman who pulls him into her bed; the aggressive women he subsequently encounters continue to be too much for him; incarceration is not a temporary way station to brilliant ascent, like Joseph's Egyptian prison, but a recurrent ineluctable fate engendering in the narrative an irreparable break before the planned final episode of liberation. Fielding, encouraged by Anglican homiletic tradition, sees the biblical characters as morally exemplary figures, even if he also satirically complicates the representation of his contemporary Abraham. Kafka, projecting a protagonist out of his own richly layered sense of personal inadequacies and imagining a world more convoluted and more resistant to human agency than that of the Bible, makes his characters swerve or fall away from their biblical models, and does not hesitate to reverse the biblical plots to which he alludes.

Kafka's writing undermines any sense that the Bible is a fixed source of authority or a reliable guidebook. For him the Bible has become a fluid entity, the components of the biblical corpus imagined in restless circulation, doubling back on one another, challenging or unsettling one another, and sometimes challenged by texts beyond the canonical corpus. The effect produced by his imagining biblical patterns in a contemporary setting is whimsical, sometimes vaguely grotesque, at moments deliberately absurd. And yet, the canon continues to confront him, to address him, to demand that he make sense of his world through it. In *Amerika* he proceeds from the assumption that the Bible can provide him a resonant structure of motifs, themes, and symbols to probe the meaning of the contemporary world. If his existential doubt, his perception of a labyrinth of contradictions in both the text and the world, are modernist, his urgent engagement in Scripture is traditional. "Turn it over and over, for everything is in it" is a maxim to which at least sometimes he might well have subscribed, though always with the proviso that some of what he turned up in turning it over might subvert the Bible's own explicit affirmations, and certainly those of most readings presupposing its canonical standing.

3
Haim Nahman Bialik
Superimposed Worlds

The Dead of the Desert
H. N. Bialik

Not pride of young lions and their dams hides the
hue of the plains,
not the oaks of Bashan—their glory mightily
fallen.
Giants lie stretched in the sun, beside their dark
pavilions,
on the yellow dunes of the desert, in lion-like
somnolence.
Massive bones hollow the sand, huge bodies
sprawl,
burly, encased in their armour, riveted in sleep to
the ground:
flint swords for their pillow, spears by the broad
shoulders,
arrow shafts at their belts, lances stuck in the sand.

Their heads are prone on the ground, their hair a dishevelled growth
matted like the tangled mane of the desert lioness.
Their faces are tough and tanned, like tarnished copper their eyes,
prey to the howling wind, game for the flame of the sun.
Their foreheads are stubborn and bold, defying the wrath of the heavens,
dangerous the bend of their brows where terrors lurk in ambush.
Their beards curl serpentine, coiled like a nest of snakes
but solid as quarried flint. Their mighty chests thrust forth —
iron anvils for time's sledge hammer — as if in eternity forged
by immense, unfathomed power now fallen eternally silent.
Only the scars on seared faces, the weals on bared breasts,
the chipping of arrow and javelin, the carved hilts of the swords
remain, like inscriptions on tombstones, to tell the descending eagle

Haim Nahman Bialik

how many lances split, how many arrows
   splintered
upon those adamant hearts, those rocks of flint.

And the sun rises and sets, whirls in its jubilees;
the desert subsides and stirs, the silence returns as
   before.
Cliffs lift their heads in wonder at the dark abyss
   of time,
arrogant in their silent splendour, proud, eternally
   alone.
For league upon league no voice, no syllable
   breaks the stillness;
oblivion has swallowed forever the victories of a
   bold generation.
Whirlwinds have razed the footprints of the
   terrible warriors of the wasteland,
sand has piled up around them, rocks thrust out
   through the dunes;
the desert holds its breath for the brave sunk in
   endless sleep.
Hot winds have eaten their strength, their glory is
   parched and congealed,
hot sands have honed flint blades to the sharpness
   of a knife-edge;

Haim Nahman Bialik

the blazing stare of the sun catches their lances'
   flash,
kindles a thousand glints on their faces' burnished
   bronze.
Exposed to the glare of the sun they are perished
   in their generations,
their vigour sapped by the east wind, dispersed
   by the southern gales
as earth that is crumbled to dust and trampled by
   pigmy feet.
Dogs lick their desiccate strength, their mighty
   power decayed.
The living dogs swallow their spittle. The
   lion-men are forgotten —
fallen and silent for ever on the yellow dunes of
   the desert.

Sometimes a sudden shadow floats across arid
   sands,
hovers and glides and soars in weaving or
   wheeling flight
to the edge of the carrion camp, and trembles
   over the dead.
Suddenly it stops in its course above the prone
   cadavers,

Haim Nahman Bialik

blackening with its dark shadow one body and
the half of another,

shaking the startled air with beating, flailing
wings:

the predator stoops to his prey, the great bird
alights.

Born and bred among rocks, hook-beaked and
crooked of claw,

he readies his iron talons against their breasts of
flint,

his long beak sharp against their obdurate faces.

A moment more and the eagle will mangle the
iron carcase,

but the bird in sudden recoil sheathes his
menacing weapons,

cowed by majestic composure, the grandeur of
drowsing might.

With great wings wide outstretched, readied to
ride the air,

a downbeat wafts him up and straight for the sun
he climbs,

thrusting into the blue till he is lost in meridian
light.

Caught on the point of a spear one quivering
feather remains,

Haim Nahman Bialik

a bright gleam, till orphaned, abandoned,
    unnoticed it falls to the ground.
And the silence creeps back as before to the
    magnificent dead.

Sometimes when the desert swoons in the heat of
    the sultry noon,
a speckled serpent glides forth, grained like a
    winepress beam,
to bask in the sun, and cosset its soft smooth rings
    of flesh;
to coil itself in the sand, languid and motionless,
melting in tender pleasure in the brilliant
    abundance of light,
waking at times to stretch and draw himself out to
    the warmth,
gape at the light, and flaunt the gold of his scaly
    coat—
the pampered pet of the desert, enjoying his
    lonely state.
Sometimes suddenly stirring, he slides from his
    lair and slithers,
sinuous, oblique and seductive across the burning
    sand
towards the camp of cadavers. He halts his
    sibilant glide,

Haim Nahman Bialik

rears his freckled height—a column of
   hieroglyphs—
raises his golden crest, tightens his throat, eyes
   alert,
and surveys from end to end the camp of the
   slumbering foe:
a multitudinous host, a numberless, infinite
   throng—
faces bared to the heavens, wrath in the arc of
   their brows.
Green flash of the ancient hatred kindles in the
   viper's eyes,
and a shudder of rage surges through him, from
   head to twitching tail
as he seethes, shaking and swaying,
poised like a rod of anger over the prostrate slain.
he slants his cruel asp head, exhales a furious hiss,
darts forth the forked black tongue fierce in its
   flickering force.
Suddenly he recoils, the serpent withdraws his
   head,
cowed by majestic composure, the grandeur of
   drowsing might.
He reverses his whole arched length, slides
   around and away—

Haim Nahman Bialik

is a whisper, a glimmer lost, in the pale bright
    distant light.
And the silence creeps back as before to the
    magnificent dead.

When nightfall and moonlight possess the bitter
    wilderness,
and a mantle of black and white conceals and
    reveals the waste,
vast stretches of sand vanish in pallid light,
louring shadows crouch at the thighs of the lofty
    cliffs,
like gigantic primordial beasts with ancient ivory
    tusks,
gathered by night to brood in silence on mystery,
at dawn to rise and lurch to the world from
    whence they came.
The sorrowful shape of the moon pours down its
    hidden light,
reflects the three-fold riddle: desolation, the night
    and the past.
The desert moans in its dream of the cruelty of
    eternal waste,
in dumb ululation wails.
Then sometimes a lion leaps forth, superb in his
    spirited strength,

Haim Nahman Bialik

strides by in stately assurance, till he comes on
the camp and halts;
raises his arrogant head, rears his majestic neck,
and the two glowing coals of his eyes scan the
camp of the foe:
an immense far-flung encampment folded in
stillness profound,
not a quiver of eyelash or hair where the mighty
lie silent, numb,
in the stripes of their spears' black shadows
seemingly shackled and bound.
The moon has silvered fierce faces and darkened
their craggy brows —
the lion pauses in wonder at the grandeur of
drowsing might.
Then tosses his shaggy mane as he utters a
bellowing roar.
League upon league around, the desert quakes
with the clamor
as it crashes and bursts among cliffs and the
canyons of silent mountains,
reverberates in a hundred thunders to the very
edge of the plain.
And the jackal responds to the voice, the hoot of
the owl replies,

Haim Nahman Bialik

the wild ass's bray rasps out, and the desert fills
with alarm
for that is the wail of the waste, the bitter lament
of the land
as it wakes in its chains to hunger, weary and
desolate.
The lion pauses a moment, ponders his
thunderous power,
turns from the carrion and departs, haughty and
calm as before;
with imperial tread he goes, tossing his royal
mane,
a torch of contempt in his eyes as he paces
proudly away.
For a while the desert still murmurs, restless and
yearning for solace—
groans in unease and sighs, and tosses in fretful
torment.
At daybreak, worn and exhausted, sleep closes its
wakeful eyes,
but a sleep that is fretted to nightmare by the
touch of the bitter dawn.
The moon grows faint and dim, light breaks at the
pale horizon,
shadows dissolve, melt down from the terraced
slopes of ravines

Haim Nahman Bialik

revealing gorge and summit livid in sullen rage.
The desert shudders to silence, awed by
   precipitous heights,
fumes again, inwardly mutters, utters a surly
   growl —
till the sun rises once more, and eternal silence
   creeps back
to the changeless magnificent dead, and the
   jubilees whirl in their round.

Sometimes the desert rebels against immutable
   silence,
rises in insurrection to avenge its desolate state,
breaks out in tempests, and raises pillars of
   whirling sand,
defies its Maker's fiat, would harry him from his
   throne,
would capsize the world to his face, and hurl it at
   his feet,
cry havoc, confusion, upheaval, till chaos come
   again.
Then the Maker is moved to wrath and the face of
   heaven changes:
a deluge of foaming fire spills on the mutinous
   desert,

blood-red from a molten cauldron, a billowing,
   boiling flood
inflaming the whole world's space, singeing the
   furthest alps.
The desert roars in its rage as it rolls in the fiery
   gulf,
and from bottomless pit to pole all is embroiled in
   confusion:
lions, tigers, blown round in the hurricane's
   whirling wind
stampede, lashed by the blast, their manes
   stiffened with fear,
headlong they rush, panic-crazed, their eyes
   flashing sparks,
seeming to fly through the air, by the clamour
   convulsed and confounded.
In that hour
seized by a vibrant impulse the mighty phalanx
   awakes.
They suddenly rouse themselves, the stalwart
   men of war,
lightning ablaze in their eyes, their faces aflame,
   hands on swords.
They raise a great shout with one voice, the voice
   of the six hundred thousand,

Haim Nahman Bialik

a voice that tears through the tumult, vies with
    the desert's roar.
Encompassed by furious storm, resolute,
    unyielding, they cry:

"We are the brave!
Last of the enslaved!
First to be free! With our own strong hand,
our hand alone,
we tore from our neck
the heavy yoke.
Raised our heads to the skies,
narrowed them with our eyes.
Renegades of the waste,
we called barrenness mother.
On the topmost crags,
among levelling clouds,
we drank from the fount
of the eagle's freedom
and who shall command us?
In the desert imprisoned,
to misery abandoned
by an avenging God,
a mere whispered song
of defiance and revolt

Haim Nahman Bialik

stirred us to rise.
To arms, comrades!
Seize sword and lance,
spear and javelin — advance!
Heaven's rage defy
and in storm reply.
Since God denies us,
his ark refused us,
we will ascend alone,
outface his wrath,
the lightning's path.
We will overcome
these impregnable hills,
meet the foe face to face.
To arms!
The storm calls: Dare!
Take lance, take spear.
Let the mountains break up,
the hills collapse,
or our bodies lie heaped
corpse upon corpse.
Onward to the hills
arise, ascend!"

Formidable the desert that moment, and who
    could subdue it?

Haim Nahman Bialik

But fear sounded out of the storm, a strange
    lamentation
as the desert wrought in its heart its own
    destruction,
a calamity cruel and bitter. Enormous ruin.

The storm ends. The desert is quiet, its wild fury
    assuaged.
Brilliant and clear is the sky, the silence
    unbroken, profound.
Traders of a caravan in transit, caught on its way
    by the storm,
rise from the posture of prayer as they bless the
    name of their God.
Somewhere here in the desert lie the six hundred
    thousand,
an eerie light on their faces: atoned in death with
    their God.
No one on earth knows the site, nor knows of
    their rise, or their fall.
Heaps of hills piled up by the storm enclose and
    encircle them.
Yet sometimes a rider of courage will leave a
    caravan trail,
spur his mettlesome horse and sail through the
    sea of sand.

Haim Nahman Bialik

Firmly astride his steed he flies like a
　　swift-winged bird,
hurls his javelin and catches it as he gallops at full
　　career;
it seems he might cleave the bright blade in his
　　hurtling impetuous speed
as he chases the weapon and grasps it, and again
　　tosses it free.
The pair disappear in the distance, the horse races
　　ahead
bearing his rider onward to a summit above the
　　clouds,
where suddenly he shies and recoils, arches his
　　neck and rears.
The rider, astonished, stares, shading his eyes
　　with his hand,
then hurriedly sheers away, the fear of the Lord
　　on his face,
violently strikes his mount and like arrow from
　　bow speeds back,
catches up with his comrades, and describes that
　　soundless scene.
The listening Arabs fall silent, and wonder among
　　themselves,
awaiting the word of the chieftain, the elder, the
　　holy one.

Haim Nahman Bialik

He raises his hand and says: "Bless the name of
    the Lord, believers,
by the beard of the prophet, by Allah, you have
    seen the desert's dead.
That is the camp of God's people, an ancient and
    valiant race,
courageous, intrepid and hardy as the Arabian
    rock.
They embittered the soul of their prophet and
    even provoked their God.
So he closed them in among mountains; doomed
    them to eternal sleep;
appointed the desert to preserve them, a memorial
    for all generations.
Allah forbids his faithful to touch even the hem of
    their robes.
Once an Arab removed a thread from the fringe
    of one of their cloaks —
his body dried up at once, till he restored it and
    made amends."
Then the elder completed his speech:
"These fathered the People of the Book."

The Arabs attend and are mute, the awe of God
    on their faces,
quietly go to rejoin their heavily laden beasts;

Haim Nahman Bialik

[113]

their robes gleam white a long while until they
    finally vanish.
The camels' humps slowly sway as they disappear
    into the distance
as if they carried away nothing more than another
    old legend.
And the silence creeps back as before to the
    barren and desolate waste.
    —*Translated by Ruth Nevo*[1]

*T*he poetry of Haim Nahman Bialik is a fascinating object lesson in how a writer's work can remain untouched by the formal innovations of modernism and yet partici-pate in the modernist spiritual project of a radical interrogation of values—what Lionel Trilling, in a telling phrase, described as "an experiment in the negative transcendence of the human."[2] Bialik was born in Russia in 1873 and died in Vienna (where he had gone from Tel Aviv for medical care), in 1934. Eight years younger than Yeats, nine years older than Joyce, he came of age at the great mo-ment of modernist ferment in European literatures. In Russia around the turn of the century, when he began to produce his greatest poems, the domi-nant trend in poetry was Symbolism, very soon to

be followed by the antithetical reaction of Acme-
ism. Although Bialik, as one recent study has argued, may have been a good deal more attentive to
Russian Symbolist poetry than most Hebrew critics have allowed, formally and in some ways thematically he is steeped in the age of Lermontov
and Pushkin.[3] His sumptuous evocation of a radiant
childhood world wedded with nature from which
he feels exiled as an adult has encouraged critics
to call him a neo-Romantic and, justifiably, has invited comparisons with Wordsworth. The best of
his lyric poems are miracles of allusive density and
intricately orchestrated image and sound, but they
display nothing of the formal disjunctions, the surprising and disorienting developments of figuration
and structure, that one associates with modernist verse. The longer narrative poems — Bialik used
the loose Russian generic label *poema* to categorize
them — exhibit studied qualities of structural coherence and choreographed formality nothing like
the aggressive disruptions of the characteristic long
modernist poem. And yet, as a product of the world
of Jewish tradition who encyclopediacally incorporated the three millennia of its literature, as a
refugee in late adolescence from the great yeshiva at
Volozhin into European modernity, Bialik took the

measure as very few other writers did of the abyss of modernity—the term (*tehom* in his Hebrew) is a central trope of modernist writing, from Andrei Bely to Joseph Conrad to the historian Gershom Scholem—and, conversely, he used the imaginative and conceptual vocabulary of modernity to challenge the values of tradition. The very fact that he wrote in Hebrew—and, in his *poemot,* a predominantly biblical Hebrew—made this challenge peculiarly radical, for the poetry in effect reconstitutes the linguistic cell structure of the tradition, reassembling the minute verbal components of the founding texts, suffused as they are with historical and theological associations, in configurations that express an antithetical vision of God, time, nature, and humanity. "The Dead of the Desert," which in one sense is his most thoroughly biblical poem, is also one of the modern texts that most drastically disrupts the canonical authority of the Bible —by forging out of the biblical materials themselves a compelling counterworld to that of the Bible.

Sometime during 1901 Bialik was invited to compose a poem using materials from Jewish legend for a new Hebrew periodical, *Small World,* a magazine intended for young readers. The project for youthful consumption rapidly generated a momentum of its own, and the 234-line poema Bialik produced, scarcely suitable for young readers, was published in the important Odessa Hebrew literary journal *HaShiloaḥ* in the spring of 1902. The mythopoeic horizon to which Bialik's language as well as his reading of certain recent Symbolist mythic poems had swept him is a vivid illustration of Gershom Scholem's meditation on the spiritual risks of the revival of Hebrew in his open letter to Franz Rosenzweig of 1925. "The power of the language is bound up in the name, and its abyss is sealed within the name. Having conjured up the ancient names day after day, we can no longer suppress their potencies. We roused them, and they will manifest themselves, for we have conjured them up with very great power."[4] In 1902 the twenty-eight-year-old Bialik living in Odessa was certainly not speaking Hebrew, which is partly what Scholem, writing two decades later in Jerusalem, had in mind when he spoke of conjuring up ancient names, but the Hebrew of the classical texts lived as vibrantly, and as urgently, in the imagination of this Yiddish-speaking poet as the most dynamic vernacular. Let us consider the opening verse-paragraph of the poem, in Ruth Nevo's fine translation, which creates an admirable English approximation, aptly Miltonic in register, of the grandeur and the high poetic decorum of Bialik's Hebrew:

Not pride of young lions and their dams hides the
    hue of the plains,
not the oaks of Bashan—their glory mightily
    fallen.
Giants lie stretched in the sun, beside their dark
    pavilions,
on the yellow dunes of the desert, in lion-like
    somnolence.
Massive bones hollow the sand, huge bodies
    sprawl,
burly, encased in their armour, riveted in sleep to
    the ground:
flint swords for their pillow, spears by the broad
    shoulders,
arrow shafts at their belts, lances stuck in the
    sand.
Their heads are prone on the ground, their hair a
    dishevelled growth
matted like the tangled mane of the desert lioness.
Their faces are tough and tanned, like tarnished
    copper their eyes,

Haim Nahman Bialik

[118]

prey to the howling wind, game for the flame of
   the sun.
Their foreheads are stubborn and bold, defying
   the wrath of the heavens,
dangerous the bend of their brows where terrors
   lurk in ambush.
Their beards curl serpentine, coiled like a nest of
   snakes
   it solid as quarried flint. Their mighty chests
   thrust forth —
   on anvils for time's sledge hammer — as if in
   eternity forged
   y immense, unfathomed power now fallen
   eternally silent.
Only the scars on seared faces, the weals on bared
   breasts,
the chipping of arrow and javelin, the carved hilt
   of the swords
remain, like inscriptions on tombstones, to tell the
   descending eagle
how many lances split, how many arrows
   splintered
upon those adamant hearts, those rocks of flint.

Bialik's Hebrew is splendidly biblical — in the
poem as a whole, he avails himself of a postbiblical

term perhaps once in twenty lines, as in this opening passage only the rabbinic word for hammer, *qurnas*, diverges from the biblical high-poetic diction. Yet the imagined world of the poem is immediately palpable as a radical transformation of its biblical source. In Numbers 14, after ten of the twelve spies sent out by Moses report that the promised land is unconquerable, God dooms the whole generation to perish in the wilderness before its offspring will be permitted to enter the land. The people's rebellious response, following upon the death of the ten spies, is to attempt to "go up to the mountaintop," to take the land by force. Moses warns them that God and the Ark of the Covenant are not with them, and their assault ends when they are wiped out by the Amalekites and the Canaanites. The other narrative kernel for Bialik's poem is a talmudic legend (*Baba Batra*, 73), four words of which are cited as an epigraph, *t'a ahavei lakh meitey midbar*, "come let me show you the dead of the desert," and which is introduced as a concluding frame of the poem: an Arab wayfarer comes upon the dead of the desert, reaches out to take a fringe of one of their garments, and shrivels up until he restores the taboo object to its place. (In the talmudic source, it is the rabbinic sage Rabba bar bar Hana who grasps the fringe and is counseled to put it back by an Arab companion. For reasons that will become evident, Bialik did not want to include a representative of postbiblical Judaism in his poem, and the universalizing force of his myth was strengthened by making another people, indigenous to the region, the sole witness at the end to the awesome power of the desert dead.) This anecdote provided Bialik the hint for imagining the dead of the desert as monumental figures in the sand, dangerous, untouchable, and frozen in time by God's wrathful doom. What he does, however, with these narrative materials is in no sense a midrashic elaboration or fleshing out of them—one might note that the classical midrash on Numbers 14 in *Bemidbar Rabbah* is actually very terse about the dead of the desert and identifies didactically with the negative view of them in the biblical text. Here instead, the poet deeply imagines a strong counterversion of the whole biblical episode, transforming it into an original myth.

The tension between two drastically disparate worlds is inscribed in the very prosody of the poem. The poem is composed in dachtylic hexameters, the meter of the classical epics, the Hebrew of course pronounced in the Ashkenazic accent that was used by European Jews, with the stress on the penultimate syllable of most words. (Bialik, his ear tuned by Russian verse, was the pioneer in introducing accentual syllabic poetry in Hebrew.) But as the Hebrew critic A. M. Lifshitz pointed out more than sixty years ago, there is a second, hidden meter shadowing the hexameters: the caesura encourages the division of lines into approximately symmetrical halves; the biblical diction encourages semantic parallelism; and Bialik's youthful experience of listening in synagogue to Torah cantillation, in which most words are stressed on the last syllable, in accordance with the Masoretic accent marks, would have enabled him to hear a second set of stresses, a second rhythm, in the Hebrew words.[5] Thus there are a good many lines that exhibit perfect biblical poetic parallelism and can be scanned two ways:

Their faces are tough and tanned, (A)
    like tarnished copper their eyes, (B)
prey to the howling wind, (A)
    game for the flame of the sun. (B)

As a hexameter, this scans:

'ázim poneýmo ushezúfim / ve'éynom kenehóshes
    mu'ámoh
míshaq livraq hítsey shémesh / u'mtfga' lerúah zilófos.

Haim Nahman Bialik

[122]

As biblical poetic parallelism, with three stresses in each verset, it reads smoothly as follows:

ʾazím panéymo uṣhezufím
  v'eynám keneḥóṣhet muʿamáh
miṣháq livraq ḥítṣey ṣhémeṣh
  umifgáʿ lerúaḥ zilʿafót.[6]

This superimposition of meters is the phonetic trace of a superimposition of worlds. The language, as we have noted, is biblical—the Job poet and the author of *Shirat Ha'azinu,* Moses' valedictory poem (Deuteronomy 32), would have had no trouble understanding it—and the ghostly echo of the formal vehicle of biblical poetry can be heard in many of the lines. And yet this is a biblical landscape in which a radical transvaluation of values has been effected. (Bialik in 1902 would have been keenly aware of the powerful influence of Nietzsche among younger Hebrew writers, even though consciously he was not ideologically aligned with this group. If, as a dutiful disciple of Ahad Haʿam, he opposed the rejection of the traditional Jewish value system by M. D. Berdichevsky and the other Hebrew Nietzscheans, the imaginative momentum of his poem carried him into an iconoclastic revisioning of values that they easily could have embraced.)

That process of transvaluation begins with the very form of the poem, its generic impetus, and its implicit conception of the function of poetry. The parallelism of biblical verse here is, after all, no more than a formal reminiscence dominated by the hexameters—the meter of the Iliad and the Aeneid. "The Dead of the Desert" resembles the martial epics of antiquity in its celebration of the fierce resolve, the immense strength, and the indomitable will of a heroic age's warriors, huge figures who dwarf the men of later times. In keeping with this high valuation of the exertion of human power through the body and its material implements, the poetry is elaborately descriptive—so much so that one critic, Yosef Ha-Efrati, argued, with a good deal of polemic exaggeration, that the proper generic rubric was "descriptive *poema*"—proceeding through the nice observation of visual detail and calling on a profusion of overlapping, mutually reinforcing terms.[7] This impulse to embrace the plenitude of the material world is alien to biblical poetry, just as the celebration of the heroic is by and large excluded from biblical literature, apart from a few fleeting gestures toward it in the Book of Samuel.

Haim Nahman Bialik

(Characteristically, in the Bible's martial poems, such as the Song of the Sea and David's victory psalm at the end of 2 Samuel, it is God and not any human who figures as the triumphant warrior.) These monumental images of mighty men of war are precisely what the biblical writers took pains to exclude from their imaginative landscape.

"The Dead of the Desert," however, is more than a latter-day heroic poem, for it sets its looming figures in a cosmic perspective, realizing through the quasi-biblical vehicle that fusion of poetry and myth to which many writers of the early twentieth century aspired. All the events of the poem are seen quite literally and relentlessly under the aspect of eternity. "Their mighty chests thrust forth— / iron anvils for time's sledge hammer—as if in eternity forged / by immense, unfathomed power now eternally silent." These very lines also provide a local intimation of one of the controlling themes of the poem—the sense of ferocious *opposition* between these heroic dead and time, the elements, God Himself. The dead of the desert in this opening passage are associated with the dangerous beasts of the wilderness—eagle, snake, and lion—which in the next three episodes will threaten to assault them and then withdraw in terror or awe. Even in monumental death, they continue to resist the blows of time and to challenge the God Who has imposed upon them His dire decree: "Their foreheads are stubborn and bold, defying the wrath of the heavens." (The literal sense of the last Hebrew phrase is "and against the heavens they are aimed.") A small but instructive instance of the shift of values embodied in the poem is the extraction from the realm of moral judgment and the restoration to literal origins in the physical realm of a biblical idiom—it occurs in Ezekiel 3:7—with a moral valence, "hard foreheads" ("stubborn" in Nevo's version), exactly like the idiom "their faces are tough" (*'azim paneymo*) two lines above, which ordinarily means "impudence." The foreheads are hard, the faces tough, because they pose a flinty resistance to the assault of the universe against them. The world of the poem is a world at war: the ancient heroes cling to their many weapons, while time, the weather, past foes, perhaps God, split countless lances and arrows against their adamant hearts.

The body of the poem comprises four narrative episodes. First, the fierce eagle descends from the clouds on the stony corpses, only to retreat suddenly with mighty wingbeat to the sky. Then the snake slithers from his lair to the field of the dead:

Green flash of the ancient hatred kindles in the
    viper's eyes,
and a shudder of rage surges through him from
    head to twitching tail
as he seethes, shaking and swaying,
poised like a rod of anger over the prostrate dead.

But the snake, too, slips away from the dead he
dares not touch. Finally, in a switch from blazing
noon to spectral moonlight, a lion approaches the
dead, his eyes a smouldering glow, pulls up short
like his two predecessors, emits a roar that splinters
the still of the desert to the edge of the horizon, and
departs. The desert itself is left restless by this dis-
turbance, "groans in unease and sighs, and tosses in
fitful torment," a condition that sets the stage for the
phantasmagoric fourth episode, the eruption of the
desert storm. The storm is represented in strongly
apocalyptic terms:

Sometimes the desert rebels against immutable
    silence,

.   .   .   .

defies its Maker's fiat, would harry him from his
    throne,
would capsize the world to his face, and hurl it at
    his feet,

cry havoc, confusion, upheaval, till chaos come
again.

In the midst of the storm, the dead rise to life,
seize their weapons, ringingly voice their defiance
of the vengeful God Who has imprisoned them
(they speak not in hexameters but in short, irregu-
lar lines), and urge each other to charge up the
mountain and conquer it. This is precisely what
their counterparts in Numbers 14 do, but in the biblical text the impregnable heights are unambigu-
ously the mountains along the eastern perimeter of
the land of Canaan, whereas the lines here suggest
a strong second sense that the heights are also the
dwelling place of God, Whose dominion the rebels
challenge:

To arms!
the storm calls: Dare!
Take lance, take spear.
Let the mountains break up,
the hills collapse,
or our bodies lie heaped
corpse upon corpse.

The storm with its apocalyptic vision comes to an
end, and the dead return to their eternal immobility.

Haim Nahman Bialik

In a kind of epilogue, a horseman from an Arab caravan gallops up to the edge of the camp of the dead, flees in panic, and then listens to the talmudic tale of the wayfarer who encountered the dead that is recounted by way of explanation by an old Arab sage traveling with the caravan.

Nothing reflects the radical thrust of the poem more strikingly than the effort of one persistent trend in Hebrew criticism to deflect it by reading the poem allegorically. The elegant choreography of Bialik's three animal encounters followed by the storm no doubt encouraged the hunt for allegorical meaning, and the first words spoken by the risen dead became for many an invitation to see a Zionist message:

We are the brave!
Last of the enslaved!
First to be free!

(The literal sense of the Hebrew sounds even more historically explicit: "The last generation of enslavement and the first of redemption are we.") It is perhaps understandable that the poem should have been read in this fashion on its appearance just five years after the inception of the Zionist movement, and Bialik's own commitment to Zionism was never in question. The poem was interpreted as an allegory of Jewish history: the snake, lion, and eagle were identified as the kingdoms of Egypt, Babylonia, and Rome (in midrashic typology, there are actually four historical kingdoms that oppress Israel), and the slumbering heroes were interpreted as rising from a living death of exilic existence in order to make their way by storm, implementing the Zionist revolution, back to the promised land. This reading, expressed by a variety of critics, was enshrined by Pinhas Lachover in his history of Hebrew literature in the 1930s, and, rather surprisingly, it continues to have a good many adherents. As late as 1989 Aharon Mazia tries to resolve what he thinks of as its marginal contradictions, and does not hesitate to identify the weapons of the dead heroes as the implements of Torah-learning that the Jews used as a principal resource in the Diaspora.[8] Even a critic who claims to propose a synthesis of the allegorical and mythic readings, Eliezer Schweid, ends up with an oddly Zionist allegorical emphasis: "In identifying with the desert in its rebellion, [the dead] seek only to extricate themselves from it to a land of the living that shelters in the kindness of God."[9] The poem itself offers not the slightest hint of any "kindness of God" (*ḥasdey 'El*), and although it does evoke mountain barriers, nothing really identifiable as the Land of Israel, no sunny "land of the living," appears on its harsh horizon. Still another latter-day critic, Ziva Shamir, writing in the late 1980s, attempts to sustain a concordance of multiple allegories alongside mythic readings and actually proposes that the three beasts in the poem represent, among other things, the three phases of the Haskalah, the Jewish Enlightenment.[10]

There has been an honorable line of Hebrew critics who have resisted the seductive simplifications of allegory and have seen "The Dead of the Desert" as a mythic poem. Especially strong readings have been proposed by Baruch Kurzweil, and following in his footsteps, Gershon Shaked.[11] Kurzweil, in a brief but suggestive essay, placed particular emphasis on the terror of endless time in which the dead of the desert are trapped, invoking the refrain, "And the sun rises and sets, whirls in its jubilees; / the desert subsides and stirs, the silence returns as before." Shaked aptly identifies the echo of Ecclesiastes (there are others in the poem) in "the sun rises and sets" and underscores the sense of futile cycles of repetition that this poem shares with that book: everything occurs in an iterative tense (including, I would argue against Shaked, the storm scene); nothing really can happen in this bleak cosmos in which human will is the hostage of the implacable forces of eternity.

What needs further critical articulation is the cultural stakes of Bialik's poetic project, its consequences for the canonical authority of the Bible. The poem, as we have seen, in the very fullness of its biblical language, with its biblical setting, deploys the medium of poetry in a way strikingly different from the Bible to convey a vision of existence strenuously divergent from that of the Bible in every significant regard. If the sense of time as cyclical recurrence draws on Ecclesiastes, it must be said that the outlook of that late book reflects a sharp dissent from the biblical consensus, a consensus in which time is conceived as linear, progressive, the medium for fulfillment through historical process. (Melville used a similar strategy in *Moby-Dick* of building allusively on a dissenting biblical text, Job, in order to conduct his imaginative argument with the dominant biblical theology.) Man in Bialik's poem is not the divinely designated master of a harmonious nature, as in Genesis 1 or Psalm 8, but instead has a kinship with the most feral agents of nature — the lion, the snake, and the eagle — and can scarcely avoid the condition of eternal warfare with the elements of the natural world, and implicitly, with the harsh and impassive God Who stands behind nature: the dead of the desert can never let go of their weapons, and through time immemorial the world directs its barrage of slings and arrows to break against their obdurate chests. The structure of the poem itself may even be a radical transformation of that most radical of biblical texts, Job — an encounter with three adversaries followed by the climax of a storm, but a storm, unlike the Voice from the Whirlwind, without any divine voice revealing beauty and purpose in the fierce energies of nature.[12] The major ethical corollary of this conception of reality as unending conflict is precisely the affirmation of heroic will and the adulation of the heroic stature of man. The poem's deepest imaginative kinship is not with Exodus, Numbers, Deuteronomy, or the Prophets but with the Iliad and, indeed, with Gilgamesh, in which two heroic companions with their unflinching swords defy a monstrous deity and death itself. Bialik's link with a pagan vision of reality in this poem is characteristic of a larger modernist tendency to shift the grounds of the authority of Scripture. The biblical canon was founded on the claim of monotheism to exclusive access to the truth. In modernist writing, canonical exclusion is often replaced by a reaching out to what was excluded, and in particular, to a reclaiming of pagan values for cultural consciousness.

This attachment to the assertion of heroic resolve in the face of a pitiless God and nature in turn explains the resonant resurgence of myth in Bialik's poem. The Bible, in the interests of confirming a comprehensive monotheistic worldview, famously suppressed myth, or at least attempted to do so. The vestiges of the mythology of antecedent ancient Near Eastern literatures are largely confined to poetic imagery of a primordial battle between gods (in Job, in the Psalms, and in some of the Prophets) and to an occasional brief and cryptic fragment of archaic material in the narrative books. One of these, the human-divine hybrid Nephilim (the "giants in the earth" of the King James Version) mentioned in Genesis 6, are invoked by Bialik as an apt epithet for his monumental dead heroes. This imaginative recovery of a mythical conception of the human, the very notion against which the biblical writers fought, has a kind of philosophic logic: if divine authority is arbitrary, no more than the manifestation of the indifference of the cosmos or, anthropomorphically imagined, its hostility to man, the only alternative to abject acquiescence is heroic self-assertion. It is, the poem implicitly concedes, a tragic self-assertion, for it is bound to be futile: man cannot escape from the prison house of time and mortality, or reverse the order of inexorable natural necessity, but he—the male gender is inevitable for this heroic myth without women—can at least summon the courage to stand up against the unbending forces of nature and the divine (rather like mad Ahab against the great White Whale), stoking the spark of greatness within him to a godlike glow in this somber landscape of doom.

This whole radical transformation of biblical materials, in some respects uncharacteristic of Bialik, brings him surprisingly close to his great Hebrew contemporary, Saul Tchernikhovsky, who unlike Bialik, was in fact an ideological Nietzschean. (There even may have been competitive emulation in the fact that "The Dead of the Desert" was Bialik's first, and only, poem written in hexameters, whereas by 1902 the young Tchernikhovsky, who was to become the great virtuoso of the hexameter in Hebrew, had already employed the meter with striking effect in two of his longer poems.) Tchernikhovsky's diction was predominantly biblical, with the major exception of the evocation of Jewish folk milieu in his idylls in a language reminiscent of Mendele's *nusakh* prose that exploited rabbinic Hebrew's lexical abundance. What is remarkable, however, about Tchernikhovsky's biblical language, especially given the powerful propensity of Hebrew poetry for allusion, is the relatively limited role played in it by allusion to specific biblical texts. Instead, Tchernikhovsky uses the language of the Bible, and especially the high language of biblical poetry, to constitute an alternative reality to the one articulated in biblical literature — a world of explosive vitalistic forces, pantheistic presences, constant crisscrossings between the human and the divine, in which the sacred and the aesthetic are not ultimately distinguishable. On the whole, Tchernikhovsky is a more pervasively philosophic poet than Bialik because he so repeatedly and insistently uses contextually redefined Hebrew terms drawn from the ancient sources to body forth a whole new set of ontological coordinates. In "The Dead of the Desert," however, Bialik undertook what amounts to a Tchernikhovskian project. Here, too, in the ways we have seen, a richly biblical language is used to limn a profoundly counterbiblical reality in which a radical reconstitution has been effected of the human and the divine, of nature and moral value. Instructively, Bialik, in general an intricately allusive poet, here also uses biblical Hebrew in a largely non-allusive way, for like Tchernikhovsky, he is interested not in building on the canonical text or even in wrestling with it but rather in creating an alternative world out of the biblical words. Of some 160 readily identifiable reminiscences of particular biblical phrases (there may well be more) in the 234 lines of the poem, the only ones that have properly allusive resonance, for the reason we have already noted, are the echoes of Ecclesiastes. Otherwise, the biblical phrases are drawn on for the sheer aptness of their idiomatic force, quite often set in surprising new contexts, as is the general practice of Tchernikhovsky. In some instances, as with the stiff or strong faces and the hard foreheads, moral idioms are translated back into the physical matrix in which they originated. In numerous other cases, biblical locutions used to represent God's awesome power are transferred to the heroic dead or to the desert beasts that approach them: the lion is *ne'adari bakoah,* "splendid in power" (Nevo: "superb in his spirited strength"), like God in the Song of the Sea (Exodus 15:6); the risen rebellious dead are "encompassed by furious storm" *(usevivam nis'arah)*, like the fiery theophany of God in Psalm 50:3. (To this phrase Bialik adds a parallel, original coinage that introduces an ominous tone, *usevivam niz'amah*, "encompassed by wrath.") Such usages are not, strictly speaking, polemic confrontations with their biblical sources but rather transpositions of theistic poetic language to lend force to an other-than-theistic vision of reality.

Let us see how this weaving of a new order of reality out of the language of the Bible operates in a brief, characteristic passage. Here is the description of the desert bathed in lunar light that sets the scene for the entrance of the lion:

When nightfall and moonlight possess the bitter
    wilderness,
and a mantle of black and white conceals and
    reveals the waste,
vast stretches of sand vanish in pallid light,
louring shadows crouch at the thighs of the lofty
    cliffs,
like gigantic primordial beasts with ancient tusks,
gathered by night to brood in silence on mystery,
at dawn to rise and lurch to the world from
    whence they came.

Haim Nahman Bialik

The sorrowful shape of the moon pours down its
   hidden light,
reflects the three-fold riddle: desolation, the night
   and the past.
The desert moans in its dream of the cruelty of
   eternal waste,
in dumb ululation wails.

This wilderness is, of course, extravagantly zoomorphic, but the motive for the figuration is something quite different from pathetic fallacy. (And two local gestures of personification are actually products of Ruth Nevo's translation: the Hebrew does not say "bitter wilderness" but simply "the wilderness and its crags"; and the cliffs in the original do not have "thighs" [*yereikhayim*] but merely "recesses" [*yarketayim*].) What informs the whole spooky evocation of the desert is a profound sense of the menacing incommensurateness of the world to the grasp of the human imagination. The desert—Bialik uses here a high-poetic term for it, *yeshimon*—wavers in the play of black and pale white between revelation and concealment, stretching out in vast expanses *(miley milin shel ḥol)* that are the equivalent in spatial extension to the temporal extension into unending eons troublingly invoked in the poem's refrains. The comparison of the cliffs to beasts acts as the poetic reminiscence of a mythic and also evolutionary creation story altogether unlike the one told at the beginning of Genesis. In a beautiful coinage, Bialik takes the Bible's archaic-poetic construct form *ḥayto*, "beast of" (as in *ḥayto yaʿar*, "beast of the forest," Psalm 104:20) and creates a mythological-sounding *ḥayto qeḏumim* (*qeḏumim* means something like "ancient times," and so "primordial beast" is quite apt); and the "ancient tusks" are *shenhabey bereishit*, literally, "tusks of in-the-beginning" (the first word of Genesis), "tusks of creation-time," thus intimating what the Hebrew poet Avraham Shlonsky would call in the title of one of his collections *bereishit aḥeret*, another genesis. (Altogether, Bialik evinces an uncanny ability to compose poetry in biblical Hebrew with a freedom of invention and a fidelity to idiomatic usage that make him seem as though he were a native speaker of the biblical language.) This vaguely mammothlike cliff beast that becomes a synecdoche for the entire desert is more akin to Yeats's rough slouching beast of an impending apocalypse than to any creature of nature in the Hebrew Bible, with the marginal exception of Job's Behemoth and Leviathan. The material world that in the Bible is given to man's naming, understanding, and dominion here looms in sullen, menacing otherness. The biblical writers are of course conscious of the harshness of the great wilderness that surrounds the small patches of human cultivation, but they count on God's providential protection even in the pitiless wasteland. "He found him in desert land," writes the poet of Deuteronomy 32, "in the waste of the wilderness wail *(yeleil yeshimon)* . . . and guarded him like the apple of His eye." In Bialik's Hebrew, that very phrase is turned into a verb, *yeleilil yeshimon* ("the desert moans"), extending the sense of the wilderness as a vast beast, and with all notions of divine protection excluded from this desert landscape. Finally, to conclude the haunting description, the moon pours down its "hidden light," *'or ganuz,* the term that in rabbinic legend refers to the light set aside from the first days of creation for the righteous in the messianic era. Here, quite notably, the idiom is stripped of any connotation of eschatological promise. The light is hidden because its source is elusive, because it defines the uneasy play of perception and misperception of the nocturnal wilderness scene and presides over the triple mystery that mere human mind cannot absorb, "desolation, the night and the past" ("the past" *qedumim* is the primeval time of *ḥayto qedumim*, "the primordial beasts"). All this is, indeed, a disturbingly other genesis.

Bialik, in renewing and transmuting the language of hoary antiquity in order to create a mythic poem, is keenly aware that he and his readers inhabit a dwindled, postmythic age. He provides one strong intimation of this awareness toward the end of the second verse-paragraph, when he imagines the vigor of the monumental dead

> dispersed by the southern gales
> as earth that is crumbled to dust and trampled by
> pigmy feet.
> Dogs lick their dessicate strength, their mighty
> power decayed.
> The living dogs swallow their spittle.

These lines provide a double contrast between our own realm and that of the dead titans — between giants and pygmies and between lions (to which the dead are compared at the very beginning of the poem through the well-established artifice of denying the comparison) and their biblical antithesis, dogs (see Ecclesiastes 9:4: "Better a living dog than a dead lion"). This stinging antithesis adumbrates the conclusion of the poem, the old Arab's retelling of the talmudic tale, which it seems to me is meant to express the inadequacy of human tradition, and especially monotheistic tradition, to grasp the poem's mythic story of cosmic indifference and tragic human defiance. The old man duly expresses admiration for the courage and hardiness of the desert generation, but he also unquestioningly embraces Allah's justice in imposing an eternal doom on the presumptuous rebels. His very last words betray the limitations of a pious pygmy perspective on giants: "These fathered the People of the Book." That epithet for the Jews was of course devised by Muhammad, but its ironic inappropriateness for the desert dead is patent. Whatever the history of their descendants, the dead, as they appear in the poem, have nothing to do with the Book *(ketav)*. Interestingly, Bialik does not use the newly minted idiom *'am hasefer,* "people of the book," but rather *'am haketav,* literally, "people of the writing." The choice was evidently dictated by a desire to echo in Hebrew the Arab cognate *ketab* ("book") actually used by Muhammad, but it also has the effect of foregrounding, ironically, the essential activity of culture, writing. The only writing with which these aggressively unlettered dead are associated in the poem is the metaphoric "inscription" *(ketovet)* of arrow and javelin on their faces and chests. The old man's inadequate words mark the penultimate moment of the poem. The genre of oral storytelling, with its eminently social context of campfire and caravan, stands out at the end in its inadequacy over against the cosmic reach of the epic poet who has conveyed the mythic grandeur of the desert dead. The caravan then moves on, disappearing into the distance, the tale and its pious teller vanishing, to be replaced at the very end by the impassive stillness that is the authentic eternal voice of the cosmos: "and the silence creeps back as before to the barren and desolate waste."

"The Dead of the Desert" is one of those instances in which the drive of a great poet's imagination takes him to depths perhaps not consciously intended and certainly not dictated by a deliberate ideological agenda. Bialik, follower of Ahad Ha'am and future proponent of the project of ingathering of classical Hebrew literature for the benefit of future generations, surely did not set out intentionally to "capsize the world," or the Bible, in the face of the Creator. The effect of the poem, however, was something close to that, as it became a profound expression of Bialik's perception of the world shorn of the faith of his Orthodox upbringing with no hint of the elegiac nostalgia for that lost faith which is observable in a good many of his shorter poems.

What are the consequences for cultural history when a poet who has fully incorporated the biblical canon — Bialik appears to have had the whole Hebrew Bible virtually by heart — uses its language to create a world antithetical to that of the Bible? The process of canonization, in the proper scriptural sense of the term though certainly not in its looser application to secular literature, is above all a process of sealing: only this text, or this corpus of texts, is the repository of revealed truth. Moshe Halbertal aptly summarizes the effect of this collective decision: "The sealed text not only acquires the status of exclusivity but new information can be gained mainly through interpreting the text, and the problems that arise are resolved by the text itself." [13] Jewish culture, beginning in the late centuries of the pre-Christian era, thus becomes progressively, even extravagantly, an exegetical culture. The eventual victory of the Pharisees over competing constructions of the biblical legacy, enshrined in the immense talmudic corpus produced by their direct heirs, meant that for Jews the sealed text would be mediated by a particular kind of exegesis, in the fullness of time generating exegeses of exegesis. The rule of thumb was that even schismatic movements, such as the Karaites, based their own claim on a new sort of appeal to the sealed text.

Bialik's project in "The Dead of the Desert" proves to be a radical one precisely because it transcends any merely polemic engagement with the canonical text. A paradoxical effect is involved: the language of the Bible gives Bialik the instruments of his poetic power, and the story in Numbers 14 gives him the narrative nucleus of his poem. And yet, there is no real exegetical relation to the biblical text. On the contrary, the underlying assumption of canonization that truth is arrived at by an interrogation of the sealed text has been discarded. Instead, the poet creates his own text that makes an implicit claim to *displace* the canonical text.

I should like to stress the merely implicit character of this claim as well as its peculiar power. Bialik hardly means to write a bible, or even one biblical book, that will supersede the canonical Bible. The Hebrew words of this poem, however, are suffused with both canonical authority and pre-canonical, primordially expressive power. Heaven and earth, chaos and creation, human pride and heroic assertion, the expanses of time and space, are resonantly registered in the millennia-old terms through which Bialik evokes the world of his poem. In certain ways, he plays upon the densely layered classical associations of these terms, as a more traditional Hebrew poet typically would do. More centrally and more drastically, he recontextualizes the old words to construct an imagined universe that works on different coordinates and different values from the imagined universe of the Bible. If the point of departure for his plot is taken from a canonical text, he uses the old traditions (talmudic as well as biblical) with the sort of freedom that, let us say, Euripides exercised in drawing on the fluid Greek traditions about the events following the Trojan War. He is not, in other words, bound by the textual terms of the canonical work as a truly exegetical writer would be.

The impact would have been negligible if he had gone about this task chiefly by assembling a kind of pastiche of biblical phrases. Poetic power makes a world of difference. Bialik at the peak of his biblicizing high style, as he surely was in the four great *poemot* he wrote between 1902 and 1905, was able to produce a densely textured, imaginatively inventive, formally resourceful Hebrew poetry that could rival the poetic force of the Psalmist, Isaiah, even perhaps of the Job poet. In our historically conditioned response to their canonical poetry, the appreciation of poetic force and the acceptance or at least recognition of moral and theological values are hopelessly entangled. Bialik confronts his readers with a similar order of poetic power, in a poetic vehicle deeply akin to the biblical one, for all the discernible formal differences, expressing a vision of reality that vigorously rejects the ontological assumptions of the Bible. The canonicity of the Bible is a precondition for Bialik's poem, but the boldness of the poem's original mythological gesture intimates the end of the age of exclusive canonicity, inaugurates a time of multiple canonicities. Instead of a sealed corpus of texts that is the source of all authority and the basis for all investigation of fundamental truths, any writer of genius and sufficiently embracing perspective can lay claim through the imaginative power of the writing to a kind of canonical authority: here in my work, the writer implies, is a way of seeing the world that will make you cast aside your comforting preconceptions and look hard with newly opened eyes into the knotted nexus of human life and eternity. From one perspective, Bialik's project in effect restores to the modern age the urgency of the writer's act in the early centuries of the first millennium B.C.E., when the resources of Hebrew literary art, against competing visions, were used to address audiences in just such an imperative way.

4

James Joyce
The Synoptic Canon

The Homeric outline of Joyce's *Ulysses* is richly complicated, as four generations of sedulous commentary have shown, by the most elaborate tracery of allusion to other texts, ancient, medieval, Renaissance, and modern. Some of these allusions are purely local, others recur occasionally, and a few—such as the allusions to *Hamlet* and to *Don Giovanni*—are reiterated with some frequency, helping to shape the principal themes of the novel. Viewed in the light of its allusions, *Ulysses* has the look of a grand palimpsest, in which bits and pieces of many of the major texts of the Western tradition, and an extremely generous sampling of minor ones as well, are repeatedly scribbled on top of one another. It is no surprise that the Bible should play a conspicuous role in this great roaming game of allusion, and the many invocations of specific biblical texts have been duly catalogued in the scholarly literature.[1] What should be stressed is that, unlike all the other non-Homeric allusions in *Ulysses*, the Bible serves, in a manner nearly symmetrical with the Odyssey, as a fundamental allusive matrix for Joyce's novel.

This choice may seem rather unusual for a writer of Catholic formation, though its thematic justification is fairly evident: Leopold Bloom is not only a latter-day Ulysses but, as heir—however ambiguous and amnesiac—of the Jewish legacy, he is a vehicle for the biblical vision: Bloom-Moses, giver of the moral law; Elijah ben Bloom, harbinger of the messiah; and the new messiah himself, clinging to a sincere if muddled vision of love and harmlessness in a world of old hatreds and stubborn strife.[2] Although the New Testament is invoked from time to time, the preponderance of the scriptural allusions are to the Hebrew Bible, in consonance with Bloom's Jewish background. The prominence of the Hebrew Bible also accords with Joyce's intention to yoke Hellenism (the Odyssey) and Hebraism (the literature of ancient Israel), Jewgreek and Greekjew, with Matthew Arnold himself accorded a cameo appearance in the opening pages of the novel. Joyce knew the

Bible through the Vulgate translation as well as through the King James Version, though because of Bloom's Jewishness, he also incorporates a few brief gestures toward the Hebrew original—most amusingly in the "Nighttown" scene, when Zoe the whore intones a sensual verse from the Song of Songs in the Hebrew for Bloom's benefit.

The Bible has, by and large, a different relation to the represented world of *Ulysses* than does the Odyssey. Homer's poem is the scaffolding upon which Joyce has constructed his novel, and as such it belongs to the Joycean Arranger behind the narrative rather than to the consciousness of the characters. It peeps out from the represented scenes of the novel in an intricate chain of sly and ingenious hints—like the picture of the nymph bathing in Molly's bedroom that points to the figure of Homer's Calypso, or the lemon-scented soap Bloom carries on his way to the bathhouse that serves as analogue to the *moly* that Hermes gives to Odysseus before he visits Circe. (Bathing figures prominently in Homer's Circe episode, which may have encouraged Joyce to conflate the sensuality of his lotus-eater chapter with Circe, anticipating his invocation of Circe later in the bordello episode.[3]) A great many of the allusions to the Bible, on the other hand, are consciously invoked by the characters, from J. J. O'Molloy's oratory on the figure of Moses in the offices of the *Freeman's Journal* to Bloom's recollection and sometimes hilarious scrambling of sundry biblical texts. This difference in modes of allusion to the Odyssey and to Scripture has a mimetic logic: if Homer and the Bible are the two great texts of origin for Western culture, the Anglophone Irish in 1904, with the exception of an occasional flamboyant pedant like Buck Mulligan, did not go around quoting Homer, whereas the Bible was still a common point of reference for this Judeo-Christian society (the very term had been coined a scant decade before the date of the novel's action), its more famous verses, stories, and figures textually recalled by middlebrow and highbrow alike. The question, however, in regard to our concern with the fate of the authority of Scripture, is whether a common point of cultural reference is equivalent to canonical status.

As an alternative to the image of palimpsest that I initially proposed, let me suggest a metaphor for modern culture that Joyce himself comes close to spelling out in the "Wandering Rocks" episode: a huge jumble of violently miscellaneous books heaped up in stalls and shop windows, in which lives of the saints, guides for tourists, books on beekeeping, false confessions, and softcore pornography rub bindings. Here is Stephen Dedalus, the most literary of the sundry pedestrians in this episode who amble along the book-strewn street, picking up a volume from a stall:

> Binding too good probably, what is this? Eighth and ninth book of Moses. Secret of all secrets. Seal of King David. Thumbed pages: read and read. Who has passed here before me? How to soften chapped hands. Recipe for white wine vinegar. How to win a woman's love. For me this. Say the following talisman three times with hands folded: —*Se el yilo nebrakada femininum. Amor me solo! Sanktus! Amen.*
>
> Who wrote this? Charms and invocations of the most blessed abbot Peter Salanka to all true believers divulged. As good as any other abbot's charms, as mumbling Joachim's. Down, baldynoddle, or we'll wool your wool.[4]

Although this act of browsing is not the whole story of the Bible in *Ulysses*, it does neatly illustrate the absorption of the authoritative text into a modern textual promiscuity, canon declined into claptrap. The canonical Five Books of Moses here have a dubious successor (the actual volume has not been identified) in an eighth and ninth book, which are manifestly a compendium of hocus-pocus, purportedly derived from the secrets of the Kabbalah, and practical tips for daily life. (The book belongs to the same comic commingling of disparate realms as the hodgepodge contents of Bloom's drawer catalogued in the "Ithaca" episode.) The scrambled hierarchies of value are mirrored in the scrambled language of the magic formula supposed to inspire a woman's love: *Se el yilo* looks like nonsense, though the *el* might be a marker of Spanish (two leading annotators of *Ulysses* have proposed deciphering it phonetically as Spanish *cielillo*, "little heaven."[5] *Nebrakaða* could be Spanish-Arabic for "blessed" (feminine form). Though the meaning of *Amor me solo* is evident, it seems agrammatical. And Latin *sanctus* appears with a *k* as an orthographic indication of the distortion of language that runs through the whole magic formula, except for the final *Amen*. Stephen's learned but far from coherent mind then begins to dance around the volume he holds, linking its incantations with those of a mystifying abbot Peter Salanka, who

James Joyce

[156]

has eluded scholarly identification, and with those of a certain Joachim, evidently the same Joachim Abbas quoted in Latin by Stephen back in the "Proteus" episode. The quotation from Joachim began with the words *Ascende, calve,* "go up, baldy," which are the cry of mockery that the gang of boys in 2 Kings 23 directs toward the prophet Elisha. (In payment for their rudeness they are gobbled up by bears he summons forth from the forest.) In Stephen's bemused cogitations, scriptural up is turned into contemporary down, though it could be claimed that the colloquial taunting tone of "Down, baldynoddle, or we'll wool your wool" is rather in keeping with the derisive sharpness of the boys' words in the original. And the biblical story alluded to is certainly one of the most bizarre in the canon, having prompted the early rabbis to declare, "There were no real bears nor forest," a phrase that became proverbial in Hebrew for "cock-and-bull story."

In any case, the Bible pops up here, both in the eighth and ninth book of Moses at the beginning and in the transmogrification at the end of "Go up, baldy" into "Down, baldynoddle," not as authoritative text but as a kind of textual residue, part of the flotsam and jetsam of modern culture. The world inhabited by these characters is a cita-

James Joyce

[157]

tional reality in which the citations are jumbled, drastically decontextualized, and generally do not cohere. "Music hath charms Shakespeare said," thinks Bloom in the bar of the Ormond Hotel (of course, it was Congreve who said it), and he goes on to reflect: "Quotations every day of the year" (p. 280). The snippets of Scripture circulate through this citational reality, severed from their function as ultimate source of truth, and more often than not misconstrued or misremembered.

Nevertheless, the Bible plays a distinctive role in the world of *Ulysses* that sets it apart from the brawling, untidy democracy of quotations in which it often appears to participate as no more than an equal partner with a welter of uncanonical texts, high and low. Joyce conceives the Bible and the Odyssey as the two great narratives of origin and the two great models for the trajectory of mortal life in our cultural tradition. In his view, everything ultimately derives from these two founding texts, and so their primacy for the representation and understanding of human experience is assumed from the first page of the novel—where a man bearing the name of the Hebrew prophet Malachi confronts a man bearing the name of the Greek mythic hero Dedalus—to the very end. Christian tradition, with its strong assumption of canon in the strict sense, viewed classical Greek literature typologically as a shadowy anticipation of the exclusive and comprehensive truth that would be registered in Scripture. Joyce instead imagines an intricate coordination and complementarity between the Odyssey and the Bible—more like the relation between two of the Synoptic Gospels than between, say, *Prometheus Bound* and the Passion Narrative as Milton would have imagined it. The Odyssey is a story about a man who wants to return home after a long separation, to come back to his wife and to rejoin his son. The Hebrew Bible is the story of an exiled and enslaved people that seeks to return to the land of its fathers, and once returned, is destined to resume the cycle—driven into exile, promised another return. (Homer also hints at a new cycle of departure after return in Tiresias's prophecy that Odysseus will have to wander bearing an oar until he comes to a people who will mistake it for a winnowing paddle.) The domestic plot of the Greek story reappears as national narrative in the Hebrew story. The Hellenic version gives us a chain of fabulous adventures driving homeward to the realm of quotidian conjugality. The Hebraic version depicts a kind of grand campaign, or in another light, a pilgrimage to attain the longed-for home. Penelope's bed, hewn by her husband out of a living olive tree, which is the ultimate goal and haven of Odysseus's *nostos,* is neatly coordinated in Joyce's synoptic vision with the land flowing with milk and honey that Moses holds forth as prospect to the Israelites struggling through the wilderness.

In the imaginative texture of the novel, these two canonical texts, in keeping with their synoptic presentation, are typically interwoven rather than made to alternate. Occasionally, Joyce does the interweaving schematically in order to provide an explicit signal of the conjoining of Hebraic and Hellenic, as when Bloom, in "Ithaca," recalls that Molly "had more than once covered a sheet of paper with signs and hieroglyphs which she stated were Greek and Irish and Hebrew characters" (p. 686). (In the national schema of the novel, Irish is a middle term between Greek and Hebrew: in "Aeolus," the conventional rhetorical trope of Ireland as the new Israel is invoked; in "Ithaca" Irish is the equivalent of Greek, Stephen's Japheth to Bloom's Shem.) Joyce's more characteristic coordination of Hebrew and Greek sources is supple, inventive, and ingeniously allusive, vigorously participating not merely in a scheme of meaning or symbolic assertion but in the realized experience of the novel. Elsewhere, I have proposed that much of the high fun of reading *Ulysses* is generated by the way we are invited to play mental leapfrog with the characters in following their jumps of association in the stream of consciousness.[6] This account, however, may suggest a purely individual and psychological impulse in Joyce's associative method: in reading Bloom, for example, we "assemble" his character from the sentence fragments and the seeming disjunctions of his mental life, identifying his characteristic dreams and quirks and obsessions, the moments of euphoria and the family traumas that he repeatedly recalls. But there is also a cultural impetus in Joyce's rapid shuttling between images, which often prove to have an important allusive dimension even as they manifest individual psychology; and the perception of these constant crisscrossings of culture is surely part of the intended imaginative pleasure of reading the novel. Let me offer two fairly brief examples.

Here are the concluding lines of the "Lotus Eater" episode. Bloom, having performed a couple of personal errands on the way, is headed for the bathhouse and contemplates in advance its pleasures:

Enjoy a bath now: clean trough of water, cool enamel, the gentle tepid stream. This is my body.

He foresaw his pale body reclined in it at full, naked in a womb of warmth, oiled by scented melting soap, softly laved. He saw his trunk and limbs riprippled over and sustained, buoyed lightly upward, lemon-yellow: his navel, bud of flesh: and saw the dark tangled curls of his bush float-ing, floating hair of the stream around the limp father of thousands, a languid floating flower. (p. 86)

Only the first two lines here are stream of consciousness. Joyce then glides into a narrator's representation of Bloom's thoughts that allows him to give them poetic shape and definition and to finely articulate the link between Homeric and biblical intertexts. Before that, the last four words of Bloom's steam of consciousness are a quotation of Jesus' words at the Last Supper. The seeming irreverence of this juxtaposition of bathhouse hedonism with the Passion story is in fact a small token of the way Joyce exploits allusions to both Testaments in order to sacralize the profane. Bloom, conjuring up the delectation of his imminent bath, affirms the wholeness, the rightness of his body as the site of simple pleasure: in the perspective of Joyce's humanism, it is as worthy an affirmation as Jesus' transcendental declaration that his body will be the vehicle of sacrifice and hence the perennial symbol of communion for believers. (Stephen's discomfort with his own body and, indeed, with the idea of bathing and its sensual associations is the counterpoint to Bloom's perception.) In what follows, Joyce's narrator executes a lovely set of psychological variations on the Odyssean motif of the chapter. Bloom's vision of immersion in the bath is a return to the warmth of the womb, the very haven he dreams of entering in his fantasies about Molly, and this notion is thus a kind of interpretation of the lotus-induced indolence in the Odyssey. The navel, the biological point of nexus with origins much contemplated in the novel, is then represented as a flower ("bud of flesh"), blurring it with the lotus flower, just as the male organ ("languid floating flower") and pubic hair ("bush") become the very lotus that is the central motif of the episode. At the same time, Bloom's penis, floating in the bath, is called "the limp father of thousands." That designation brilliantly fuses psychology with allusive typology. The organ is limp because Bloom is at rest in the bath. It is also limp because there are doubts about his virility and his future prospects of procreation. And yet, physiologically, the member in question is the conduit for countless thousands of sperm, the potential progenitor of myriads. Behind this droll notion stands a biblical text and a biblical figure: Abraham, the first father of the Hebrew people, whose name is glossed in Genesis as "father of a multitude of peoples." Bloom may be a modern sad sack, a failure as husband and father, and yet as Jew, aligned through biblical allusion with Abraham (as well as with Moses, Elijah, and the future messiah), he embodies fatherhood in the novel not only as a personal vocation but, like Abraham, as a trusting, stubbornly hopeful projection of self into posterity, a kind of spiritual calling. The beauty of the synoptic allusive maneuver is that Homer's lotus eaters, lapsing into sweet somnolence, and Abraham the patriarch, hearing the impossible promise of offspring as multitudinous as the stars, are held together in delicate suspension.

The other example I would like to consider in this connection, which belongs to Stephen's consciousness, also involves navels, wombs, and, even more emphatically, myths of origins. At the beginning of "Proteus," Stephen sees a midwife he recognizes walking along the beach and is thus led to think about birth:

> One of her sisterhood lugged me squealing into life. Creation from nothing. What has she in the bag? A misbirth with a trailing navelcord, hushed in ruddy wool. The cords of all link back, strandentwining cable of all flesh. That is why mystic monks. Will you be as gods? Gaze in your omphalos. Hello. Kinch here. Put me on to Edenville. Aleph, alpha: nought, nought one. (pp. 37–38)

This is a moment in which Stephen exhibits an exuberant athleticism of associative thinking and even a certain vernacular touch that anticipate Bloom. Despite his penchant for Latin, he renders *creatio ex nihilo* here in plain English. The only erudite term is the Greek *omphalos* for "navel," a word that has been on his mind since his early-morning conversation with Buck Mulligan. Even that, however, in the amusing game with the reader of representing consciousness, has been in effect pretranslated in the truncated predicate of "That is why mystic monks" (a sentence in style and content altogether Bloomian). The engaging conceit on which these lines turn is of course the notion of the umbilical cord as a long coil of telephone cable (still a rather new technology in 1904) linking each of us back to Eden, the ultimate place of origin. The associative field of Eden triggers the quotation of the serpent's words to Eve—in the biblical original, a declaration and not a question—"Will you be as gods?" Getting back to Eden is going home, a return to the welcoming womb of life, to woman whose womb is the bourne of the male wanderer: Stephen-Telemachos feels remorse over his dead mother and fear of woman's body; Bloom-Odysseus is also self-excluded from this paradisal place but constantly dreams of it and in the end will realize a kind of proximate return to the Ithaca of his Penelope's bed. This little segment of fantasy concludes with Kinch ("the kid," Stephen's jocular self-designation) trying to put through his call to Edenville. "Nought, nought, one," which, a century after the 1904 date on which the novel is set, sounds rather like an access code for an international call, is of course the telephonic transposition of creation from nothing. The prefix to this cosmogonic telephone number is formed by the initial letter of the Hebrew and of the Greek alphabet, aleph properly proceeding alpha as it did in time, and because the Greek was actually borrowed from the Semitic. The fact that aleph and alpha are really the same letter, with a minor phonetic difference, despite their different graphic configurations, serves Joyce's purposes beautifully, and neatly illustrates why the Hebrew Bible and the Odyssey are the two fundamental intertexts of *Ulysses*, differing in function from the many hundreds of others invoked in the novel. The encyclopedic reach of Joyce's project, so deliberately conceived as an attempt to produce a modern masterpiece, entails not only the exhaustive representation of a day in the life of an ordinary modern man but also a kind of grand recapitulation of three millennia of cultural history.[7] In this landscape of recapitulation, many important writers and thinkers loom: Aquinas, Maimonides, Dante, Shakespeare, Goethe, Flaubert, to name just a few. The logic of recapitulation, however, leads back to the ultimate point of departure, raising questions about how we derive from our distant beginnings, how we unwittingly or consciously repeat them, how we might adapt or transmute their meanings from our own belated vantage point in the great spiral of time. For this process of imaginative investigation of the Western tradition, only two bedrocks of allusion will serve — Homer and the Bible. The call back to Eden, which in the Bloom sections of the novel will be rerouted as a call back to Ithaca and/or to the Promised Land, is thus aptly prefixed by aleph and alpha. What Joyce is doing in effect is to make philogeny recapitulate ontogeny: the old Mediterranean myth of the origin of the species becomes a mirror for the origins of individual life.

From Joyce's perspective as recapitulative modernist and as expatriate Irishman, the Odyssey and the Hebrew Bible represent different inflections of a single synoptic plot. Odysseus wanders across the Mediterranean, escaping dangers and skirting temptations to make his way home. Abraham crosses the Mesopotamian Valley westward toward a new home God says He will show him, as his descendants will journey northward through the wilderness from Egyptian bondage to the land they have been promised. Both traditions of the *nostos* or voyage of return involve a linear plot forged from linked episodes in which the hero, singular or collective, through resolution and daring, takes hold of his homeland — Odysseus slaughtering the would-be usurpers, Abraham defeating the allied kings of the East as his descendants will conquer the Canaanites. Each of these ancient stories has a theological underwriting, though the Odyssey is more casual in this regard: Odysseus is guided homeward by his tutelary goddess, Athena, and of course Abraham, Moses, and the Israelites are emphatically directed and protected by the Lord of Hosts.

What is a modern person, at least as Joyce understands the nature of modernity, to make of these stories? The plot of return, the very reunion with origins implicit in the use of Homer and the Bible, is abidingly meaningful for Joyce: it explains something fundamental about how each of us feels as a creature flung into the exile of existence and sustained by the power of longing for a return to some primal unity. At the same time, Joyce is compelled to alter some of the basic terms of his two texts of origin. The background of transcendence of polytheistic Homer and of the monotheistic biblical narrative is largely absorbed into a secular foreground, though a potent residue of the sacred remains palpable in Joyce's novel: Molly may be a second-rate singer, frustrated wife of a down-at-the-heels advertising canvasser, and an eager adulteress, but the novel also conveys a sense that she really is an avatar of Calypso, Penelope, Gea-

Tellus, the Virgin Mary, and the beautiful beloved of the Song of Songs. Joyce's invocation of the Greek and Hebrew matrix-texts is thus more than a literary trick because his vision of human existence in part draws deeply on theirs, his aestheticist pantheism answering to their differing theisms. At the same time, he dissolves the linear plot of his two ancient narratives into its episodic components, for he cannot fully embrace the idea of progression in time to grand resolution, and he positively rejects the assertion of will through martial effort on which the ancient dénouements depend. (One notes that his own imaginative purchase on the ancient world is diametrically opposite to Bialik's.) His Odysseus returns home, sort of; his Moses looks down at last on the Promised Land, in a manner of speaking; for heroic fulfillment is more a teasing dream than a realizable destiny in his world. The great affirmation of his modern epic is the simple embracing of ever-renewed life and beauty, sublimely expressed in Molly's soliloquy, and intimated in a quieter key in the sense of reconciliation Bloom attains in the penultimate episode. That affirmation in turn is implicitly endorsed by both the Greek and the Hebrew intertexts, the Odyssey with its world of sparkling sunlight in which conjugal love and fatherhood are confirmed, the Hebrew Bible with its beckoning prospect of milk and honey, its urgent injunctions to be fruitful and multiply and to choose life over death.

Having stressed till now a neat equivalence in Joyce's relation to his Hellenic and Hebraic source-texts, I should add that there is also a distinction of cultural implication in his treatment of the two. The Odyssey in the Greek world enjoyed an approximate, secular canonicity, thought of as an encyclopedic reservoir of wisdom, made the object in late antiquity of allegorical and other sorts of exegesis. After antiquity, it was conceived in more strictly literary terms, however salient its role as a fountainhead of Western literature. As a work of literature, not inspired scripture, it could readily become a playground of irreverent parody and burlesque as well as an object of emulation. A purely playful, even bawdy treatment of the Bible is not unheard of in the age of faith—striking instances occur in Emmanuel of Rome, the fourteenth-century Hebrew poet—but these are no more than the exceptions that prove the rule. The rule would be that the text endorsed by divine inspiration is to be approached in an attitude of intense spiritual concentration (Kafka still does this) as the authoritative source of truth. Parody and its cousins are allowed access only in the carnivalesque moments of the religious calendar or in the carnivalesque outer precincts of the system of literary genres. Joyce, in subjecting the Bible to repeated, often exuberant parody, tacitly puts aside its claims to transcendent authority, affirming instead its purely literary canonicity, symmetrical with that of the Odyssey.

Thus, in the grand mishmash of literary jokes, burlesques, and fractured allusions that constitutes the "Oxen of the Sun," we hear: "Remember, Erin, thy generations and the days of old, how thou settedst little by me and by my word and broughtest a stranger to my gates to commit fornication in my sight and to wax fat and kick like Jeshurum" (p. 393). These words are an obvious pastiche of Moses's words of admonition to Israel in the valedictory poem of Deuteronomy 32. The momentary possibility of a serious typological correspondence between Israel and Erin is dissolved by the introduction of the fornicating stranger in the gates (not part of Deuteronomy 32), a reference to Blazes Boylan, who has recently been romping with Molly behind the closed bedroom door— Bloom's "gates"— of 10 Eccles Street. The pastiche of phrases from the King James Version continues for another dozen lines, concluding with an evocation of Moses on Mount Nebo, who like his avatar Bloom looks out on but will not enter his Promised Land, which, in a deliberately flagrant pun that turns parody into burlesque, is styled "a land flowing with milk and money."

There is a good deal—perhaps an excess—of sheer verbal horseplay in *Ulysses,* and in this regard Scripture is treated like any other text, however profane. One should keep in mind, however, the truism that every parody involves a covert admiration for the work parodied. On a purely stylistic level, Joyce revels in the eloquence of the Bible, as refracted through the King James Version. More seriously—for he is, in his own portmanteau coinage, a "jocoserious" writer (p. 677) —the Bible gives him an embracing archetypal pattern for the representation of human life. I have already touched on that aspect of the pattern which he coordinates with the Odyssey—the plot of return. Two more distinctively biblical motifs that appeal to Joyce are the idea of redemption (considerably more than an Odyssean setting of one's house in order) which is focused in the messiah figure, and the associated theme of instruction, again a Hebraic rather than a Hellenic emphasis. The early rabbis fancied the notion of "the beauty of Japheth, *yefei-fiuto shel Yafet*, in the tents of Shem"—that is, the representatives of Greek aesthetic culture coming to receive moral instruction in the study-house of the Hebrews, and Joyce seems to have been aware of this little allegory. It is enacted, in appropriately jocoserious fashion, in the exchanges between Bloom and Stephen as they wend their way to Eccles Street in "Ithaca." "What satisfied him?" the catechistic narrator asks of Bloom once the two men have sat down in the Blooms' kitchen. "To have sustained no positive loss. To have brought gain to others. Light to the gentiles" (p. 676). The biblical tag at the end invites the application of messianic instruction to Bloom's encounter with Stephen and with others he has met during his long day. This is, one must admit, messianism reduced to a quotidian horizon of very modest expectations and rendered in the bookkeeping terms (loss and gain) of Bloom's mental world. Nevertheless, as outsider in Dublin, uncircumcised Jew, fitful and often befuddled heir to Moses and the Prophets, Bloom has brought a kind of flickering dream of redemption to the world of the novel. He is prophetic in the mood of the sweet prophecies of restoration of Deutero-Isaiah that are cast in marital imagery, rather than Odyssean, most crucially in his final attitude toward the usurper, or imagined chain of usurpers, of his conjugal bed. Whereas Odysseus cleanses his palace by massacring the whole crowd of suitors, Bloom in the end restores harmony to his home by accepting his beloved wife's betrayal as a transient act of frailty under the humbling aspect of eternity. Thus he renounces all thought of retribution in a great catalogue of reasons that begins with "the preordained frangibility of the hymen" and eloquently ends with "the continual production of semen by distillation: the futility of triumph or protest or vindication: the inanity of extolled virtue: the lethargy of nescient matter: the apathy of the stars" (p. 734).

Bloom's final movement of inward reconciliation with all the imperfections of the human condition provides a serious underside to the jocularity with which the 113th Psalm is burlesqued when he leads Stephen out into the garden *(In exitu Israël de Egypto: domus Jacob de populo barbaro)*, showing the way with a candle held on high. The psalm in question is the one Dante cites in his letter to Can Grande to explain how he intends the method of fourfold layers of meaning used in the interpretation of Scripture to be applied to his *Comedy*. If the

Odyssey offers Joyce a model of life as a series of vivid and varied adventures, the Bible gives him a model, not literally believed but suggestively paradigmatic, of life as spiritual procession and induction into wisdom. Bloom, a dropout from fatherhood who dreams of paternity; a failed husband whose imagination stubbornly lingers over the joys of conjugal union; and, above all, a pacific man in a world of blind animosities, has earned his right, however ironically qualified, to be a light to this gentile.

There is, moreover, an implicit conception of history in the Hebrew Bible not shared by the Homeric epic that provides a kind of ontological warrant for Joyce's whole elaborate structure of allusion. As a reader of Vico, he was much taken with the notion that history repeats itself in cycles. The Bible structures its overarching narrative as a sequence of repeated patterns. The banishment from Eden foreshadows the banishment from the land as the enslavement in Egypt adumbrates Babylonian captivity. The crossing of the Sea of Reeds is ritually reenacted in the crossing of the Jordan led by Joshua. The two spies in Numbers who bring back an encouraging minority report have their counterparts in the two spies Joshua sends to Jericho whose intelligence helps enable the conquest. They, in turn, recur in the two spies who bring David news from Jerusalem during Absalom's rebellion and are hidden by a resourceful woman just as Rahab the harlot hid Joshua's two spies. Joyce brilliantly conjoins this idea of historical recurrence with the teasing possibility and frustrating impossibility of recurrence in an individual life. Thus Bloom, after his onanism on the strand, sadly contemplates himself as a man over the hill from love, ages removed from that rapturous moment of his youth on Ben Howth when he tasted the sweetness of seedcake and of young Molly. "The year returns," he reflects. "History repeats itself." Then, after an expression of mixed feelings about the young woman down the beach who has exposed herself to his voyeur's gaze, he flashes back on the distant experience with Molly on Ben Howth: "All quiet on Howth now. The distant hills seen. Where we. The rhododendrons. I am a fool perhaps. He gets the plums and I the plumstones. Where I come in. All that old hill has seen. Names change: that's all. Lovers: yum yum" (p. 377).

The "he" who gets the plums is Blazes Boylan, who, as Bloom is painfully aware, would have recently completed his tryst with Molly. The yum

yum of lovers recalls the enjoyment of seedcake, and other appetitive pleasures, in Bloom's early sharing of passion with Molly. "Names change: that's all" is a reflection on the endless generations of lovers that succeed one another. Behind this stands Joyce's notion that human life is, after all, an eternal cycle of recurrences: the names change, but one Leopold Bloom may also be Abraham and Moses and Elijah, while his own name hints at two biblical ones—the Lion of Judah (Leopold) and the messianic restorer whom Zechariah calls Zemach, "shoot" or "bloom." Joyce's aging wanderer then proceeds to spin out a fantasy of himself as Rip Van Winkle, returning after twenty years of absence to the transformed world of his youth, "his gun," in an arch allusion to Bloom's retreat from sexual intimacy, "rusty from the dew." It is in the midst of this reverie about returning to one's youth that Bloom invokes the somber Ecclesiastean refrain of eternal recurrence: "Nothing new under the sun." The profundity of Joyce's representation of human existence is reflected in his sense of dialectic fluctuation between irrevocable banishment from the élan of origins and recurrence, which in an individual life may turn out to be buoyant renewal. Molly's yes-saying hymn to a world of flowers at the very end bespeaks a renewal in her of the eternally recurrent excitement of first love and the embracing of life, and Bloom's flashbacks to that youthful ardor on Ben Howth serve the same purpose.

In the larger historical and cultural scheme of the novel, this dialectic is manifested in the oscillation between images of the Promised Land as a place of irreversible desolation and as a place of glorious renovation. Bloom, having discovered in the pork butcher's the newspaper with the advertisement for the Zionist society that Joyce calls Agendath Netaim, conjures up a fecund landscape of silvergray olive trees, herds of cattle, oranges packed in crates lying on the wharves. Then a cloud covers the sun, casting a gray shadow over Dublin, and triggers in Bloom an antithetical cluster of reflections. His haunting power as a poet of associative images is nowhere more palpable:

> No, not like that. A barren land, bare waste. Vulcanic lake, the dead sea: no fish, weedless, sunk deep in the earth. No wind would lift those waves, grey metal, poisonous foggy waters. Brimstone they called it raining down: the cities of the plain:

Sodom, Gomorrah, Edom. All dead names.
A dead sea in a dead land, grey and old.
Old now. It bore the oldest, the first race.
A bent hag crossed from Cassidy's clutch-
ing a noggin bottle by the neck. The oldest
people. Wandered far away over all the
earth, captivity to captivity, multiplying,
dying, being born everywhere. It lay there
now. Now it could bear no more. Dead: an
old woman's: the grey sunken cunt of the
world. (p. 61)

This is surely one of the most evocative medi-
tations on the meaning of Genesis 19 in any language. The ancient names from the biblical landscape of desolation are "All dead names," yet,
paradoxically, they are potently alive in Bloom's
imagination, just as, in a kind of fortuitous pun,
a living "bent hag" crosses his field of vision, encouraging him to see the ancient land as a with-
ered old woman. The blunt Anglo-Saxon monosyl-
lable for the female sexual part by which Bloom
figures the Dead Sea at the end is wonderfully apt,
as the metaphor at once intimates the actual shape
of the Dead Sea and the fact that it is the lowest
place on the face of the globe. The sexual image

also eloquently ties the historical into the personal. The womb, which preoccupies Bloom and Stephen alike, is both the source of fecundity and the bourne of love. The great question posed by *Ulysses*, a novel about fertility in the psychological, biological, and mythic-cultic sense, is whether the dessicated wellspring of vitality can flow again with life, whether a time-battered man and woman in the middle of their journey can recapture a sense of early passion, find a possibility of renewal in the cycle of their mortal years. In the biological sense, renewal is a mocking impossibility, as the Dead Sea, sunken forever in its saline sterility, suggests to Bloom. As a faculty of the imagination, renewal is a powerful motor force that makes it possible for the ephemeral human creature to embrace life again and again, to the very end, as eager Sancho Panza urges Don Quixote on his deathbed. This is the great burden of the soliloquy by Molly with which the novel concludes.

In all this, the canonical status of Scripture is subverted, transformed, and reaffirmed in new terms. By equating the Bible with Homer as a matrix of allusion, Joyce implicitly rejects the traditional notion of Christians and Jews that the Bible is the ultimate or even exclusive source of authority, all other texts being no more than ancillary or complementary to an understanding of its abiding truths. Joyce called his novel *Ulysses* rather than by any biblical name, placing the Homeric intertext in the foreground, because he wanted to set his ambitious modernist project in the literary context of the epic genre, inviting us to see the prosaic tribulations of his middling modern man as legitimate new versions of the high adventures of the Greek hero. But the Bible was a necessary complement to Homer in Joyce's literary scheme. It offered him an elaborate set of national equivalences for Odysseus's more personal undertakings, put into play as Homer does not the category of history itself, and introduced considerations of ethical imperatives together with a horizon of redemption. By conjoining the Bible with the Odyssey, Joyce's novel is able to take stock of the literary origins of the Western tradition and suggest how they might be relevant to a cultural future. The notion of a single authoritative canon that sets the limits for the culture is tacitly and firmly rejected, while the perennial liveliness of the old canonical texts as a resource for imagination and moral reflection is re-affirmed. In the extraordinarily supple and varied uses to which the Bible is put in *Ulysses*, it is converted into a secular literary text, but perhaps not entirely secular, after all, because it is reasserted as a source of value and vision. This is not a mode of canonicity that would have made sense to the sages of Yavneh in 90 C.E. or to the Church fathers, but for the culture based on a fusion of disparate antecedents, and of old and new, that is the aim of the more hopeful branch of modernism, it is a canonicity that can still nourish us.

James Joyce

notes

All translations are mine, except as noted.

Introduction

1. William Faulkner, *Absalom, Absalom!* (New York: Random House, 1980), p. 80.
2. Walter Benjamin, *Illuminations,* trans. Harry Zohn (New York: Schocken, 1968), p. 257.

one
The Double Canonicity of the Hebrew Bible

1. See Sid Z. Leiman, *The Canonization of Hebrew Scripture: The Talmudic and Midrashic Evidence* (Hamden, Conn.: Archon Books, 1976).
2. The Hebrew text is taken from T. Carmi, *The Penguin Book of Hebrew Verse* (New York: Penguin, 1981), p. 203. I have made somewhat related observations on this poem in my book *Hebrew and Modernity* (Bloomington: Indiana University Press, 1994), though there I used Carmi's translation.
3. The Hebrew text is taken from H. Schirmann, *Hashirah*

haʻivrit beSefarad ubeProvence (Jerusalem: Mossad Bialik, 1954), 1: 107.

4. Schirmann, *Hashirah haʻivrit*, 1: 496.

5. All translations of Genesis are from Robert Alter, trans. *Genesis: Translation and Commentary* (New York: Norton, 1996).

6. The Hebrew text is taken from Saul Tchernikhovsky, *Shirim* (Tel Aviv: Am Oved, 1990), p. 200.

t w o

Franz Kafka

1. Gershom Scholem, "Ten Ahistorical Theses on the Kabbalah," in *ʻOd Davar* (Tel Aviv: Am Oved, 1989), p. 37.

2. Franz Kafka, *Parables and Paradoxes* (New York: Schocken, 1961), p. 35. All quotations from the reflections on the Tower of Babel are from this edition.

3. *The Correspondence of Walter Benjamin and Gershom Scholem, 1932–1940*, ed. Gershom Scholem, trans. Gary Smith and Andre Lefevre (New York: Schocken, 1989), p. 243.

4. Moshe Halbertal, *People of the Book: Canon, Meaning, and Authority* (Cambridge: Harvard University Press, 1997), p. 19.

5. Kafka criticism has not really registered the centrality of biblical allusions in *Amerika*. Symptomatically, Ralf R. Nicolai's *Kafkas Amerika-Roman "Der Verschollene"* (Würzburg: Königshausen und Neumann, 1981) includes an index of motifs and themes that runs to 177 items without incorporating a single biblical text.

6. Franz Kafka, *Amerika*, trans. Willa and Edwin Muir (New York: Schocken, 1962), p. 3, translation modified. All citations from the novel are from this edition.

7. John Hollander, *The Gazer's Spirit* (Chicago: University of Chicago Press, 1995), p. 185.

8. I am indebted to Bluma Goldstein for the characterization of Kafka as an in-between person.

9. For an illuminating exposition of these motifs in Chagall see Benjamin Harshav, "Chagall: Postmodernism and Fictional Worlds in Painting," in *Marc Chagall and the Jewish Theater* (New York: Guggenheim Museum, 1992), pp. 15–60.

10. Martin Battestin, *The Moral Basis of Fielding's Art* (Middletown, Conn.: Wesleyan University Press, 1959).

three
Haim Nahman Bialik

1. Chaim Nahman Bialik, *Selected Poems*, trans. Ruth Nevo (Jerusalem: Dvir and Jerusalem Post, 1981), p. 102. All subsequent quotations of the poem are from this translation.

2. Lionel Trilling, *Beyond Culture* (New York: Viking, 1965), p. 81.

3. On Bialik and Symbolism see Esther Nathan, *Haderekh lemeitey Midbar* (Tel Aviv: Hakibbutz Hameuhad, 1993). Nathan proposes persuasive parallels between Bialik's "The Dead of the Desert" and Russian Symbolist poems by Balmont, Merezhovsky, and Solovyov,

including the motifs of titans and of heroes roused from frozen slumber.

4. Gershom Scholem, *'Od Davar* (Tel Aviv: Dvir, 1989), p. 53.

5. A. L. Lifshitz, *"Hamishqal hane'elam beshirat Bialik,"* in *Keneset* 2 (1937): 105–112.

6. My second transliteration is into the prevalent modern, or "Sephardic," pronunciation with which most people studying the Bible in Hebrew now pronounce it, and that pronunciation is faithful to the indications of stress in the Masoretic text.

7. Yosef Ha-Efrati, *"Meitey Midbar—Poema Tei'urit,"* *Hasifrut* 1:1 (1968), 101–129.

8. Aharon Mazia, *"Mered 'Meitey Midbar' vekishlono,"* in *Hallel leBialik,* ed. H. Weiss and Y. Yitzhaki (Ramat-Gan: Bar-Ilan University, 1989), pp. 171–181.

9. Eliezer Schweid, *Ha'ergah lemelei'ut hahavayah* (Tel Aviv: Sifriat Poalim, 1968), p. 38.

10. Ziva Shamir, *"Meitey Midbar: Ma'agal haqesamim shel hacosmos,"* in *'Al Meitey Midbar,* ed. Z. Luz (Ramat-Gan: Bar-Ilan University, 1988), pp. 229–252.

11. Baruch Kurzweil, *Bialik uTchernikhovsky: Mehqarim beshiratam* (Jerusalem and Tel Aviv: Schocken, 1960), pp. 82–88; Gershon Shaked, *Sifrut 'Az, K'an, ve'akhshav* (Tel Aviv: Zmora-Bitan, 1993), pp. 203–221.

12. I am indebted to Ivan Marcus for this challenging suggestion.

13. Moshe Halbertal, *People of the Book: Canon, Meaning, and Authority* (Cambridge: Harvard University Press, 1997), p. 19.

f o u r
James Joyce

1. See, for example, Virginia Douglas Mosley, *Joyce and the Bible* (De Kalb: Northern Illinois University Press, 1967).

2. On Bloom as messiah, see my essay "James Joyce's Comic Messiah," *American Scholar* 66:3 (Summer 1997), 452–461.

3. I am grateful to my friend Thomas G. Rosenmeyer for pointing out to me the connection between the two episodes.

4. James Joyce, *Ulysses* (New York: Random House, 1961), pp. 242–243. All subsequent quotations are from this edition.

5. Don Gifford and Robert J. Seidman, *Notes for Joyce* (New York: Dutton, 1974), p. 225.

6. Robert Alter, "Joyce's *Ulysses* and the Common Reader," *Modernism/Modernity* 5:3 (September 1998), 19–31.

7. On the concept of the modern masterpiece, see Michael André Bernstein's illuminating account, "Making Modern Masterpieces," *Modernism/Modernity* 5:3 (September 1998), 1–17.

Index

Christianity, 9, 158–159,
181–182; Church canon, 1;
Church fathers, 2, 183
Chronicles of the Kings of
Israel, 30
citation, 157–158
"City Coat of Arms, The"
(Kafka), 70, 77–78
comparison, denial of, 142
Conrad, Joseph, 116
creation, 24, 31, 43–44, 140,
164–167
critics, 129–132
Cultural Zionism, 55

Dante Alighieri, 26, 167, 175
David (biblical), 10, 14, 15
"Dead of the Desert, The"
(Bialik), 7, 97–114, 118–
119; canonical authority
of Bible and, 116; cosmic
perspective of, 125–126;
idiomatic Hebrew in, 140–
141; martial epics and,
124–125; myth in, 134–
135; narrative episodes of,
126–129; radical project
of, 146–149
Dead Sea, 180–181
Dead Sea sectarians, 28
deconstruction, 49
determinism, 5
Deuteronomy, Book of, 133,
141, 172
Diaspora, 130
Dickens, Charles, 79, 91
Dickinson, Emily, 33
doctrine, 33, 35, 57; canonicity and, 48, 60; canon-

izers' motives and, 4–5;
exclusion from canon and,
31; rejection of doctrinal
consensus, 27; suspension
of, 50
double canonicity, of Bible,
4, 18, 33, 148; Christian
and Jewish, 21–22; Halevi
and, 48, 50; modern
Hebrew literature and,
51; Spanish Hebrew poets
and, 40; Tchernikhovsky's
poetry and, 59
dreams, 46, 50

Eastern Europe, 33, 50
Ecclesiastes, Book of, 24,
131–132, 178; allusions
and, 137; ideology and,
28–29; poetry and, 34,
129–130
Eden, Garden of. See Garden
of Eden
Egypt, 41, 84–85, 89, 91;
allegorical representation
of, 130; exodus from, 36
Elhanan (biblical), 15
Elijah the Prophet, 164, 178
Eliot, George, 2
Eliot, T. S., 49
Emmanuel of Rome, 47, 171
English literature, 32–33
Enlightenment, 33, 50
enslavement, theme of, 85,
87, 88, 91
epic, 121, 144, 182
epithalamia, 36
erotica/eroticism, 28, 35, 46,
47

Index

Index

prosody. *See* meter
Protestantism, 94, 95
Proust, Marcel, 7–8
Proverbs, Book of, 34
Prussia, 33
Psalms, Book of, 34, 46–47, 134
psychoanalysis, 82
Purim, 27
Pushkin, Alexander, 26, 53, 115

rabbis, 2, 28, 157
Rashi, 64
rationalism, 5
read in Hebrew, 32
realism, 7, 8
recapitulation, 167, 168
redemption, 23, 173, 174, 182
Renaissance, 45, 47, 151
renewal, 180–181
repeated patterns of narrative in, 176–177
Restoration (English), 39
return, plot of, 169, 173
revelation, 65, 159
Rimbaud, Arthur, 7
Romanticism, 50
Rome, ancient, 130
Rosenzweig, Franz, 117
Russia, 26, 33, 52, 56

sacredness, 1, 4, 136
Samuel, Book of, 10, 14, 15, 124
Sanhedrin, 22
schismatic movements, 146
Scholem, Gershom, 66–67, 69, 76–77, 117; on exe-
gesis, 16; on Kafka and Kabbalah, 94; modernity and, 116
Schweid, Eliezer, 130
Scripture, 18, 32, 61, 181; authority of, 92, 133, 154; canonization of, 22–23; citation and, 158; inspired status of, 42, 47–48; playfulness and, 50; as revealed truth, 65. *See also* Bible
Second Commonwealth, 31
secularism, 59, 183
secular literary text, 182–183
sensuality, 5, 28, 153, 163
sexuality, 78–79, 93; in Joyce's *Ulysses*, 163–164, 177–179, 180–181; in Kafka's *Amerika*, 78–79, 83–84, 88
Shaked, Gershon, 131–132
Shakespeare, William, 26, 39, 167
Shamir, Ziva, 131
Shirat Ha'azinu, 123
Shirei tiferet (Weisel), 51–52
Shlonsky, Avraham, 140
Song of Songs, 24, 31, 57, 170; double canonicity of, 35–39; exceptionality of, 58–59; as popular work, 27, 28; secular poetry and, 34; *Ulysses* (Joyce) and, 153
Song of the Sea, 125, 137
Songs of Glory (Weisel), 51–52
sonnets, 57–58

Index

[197]

Index